"Lindsay Gibson's book is treasure trove of gol[
cal insights, wisdom, and inspiration written
experienced professional who has a deep unde
tion. As the child of two emotionally immature [, ...ts, I felt the book was
a window into my soul reaching in, offering me a hand and lifting me up."

>—**Arlene Ingram**, retired PK-12 school counselor with thirty-five
> years' experience; and former president of the Virginia Counselors
> Association, and of Potomac and Chesapeake Association for
> College Admissions Counseling

"Lindsay has done it again! *Self-Care for Adult Children of Emotionally Immature Parents* is the loving advice and instruction that those of us with these types of parents needed but never got. Lindsay offers compassion with application for guiding us on how to reparent ourselves, while throughout, reminding us that we deserve to have better lives! This book is another Lindsay Gibson 'must-have' in everyone's library."

>—**Ameé Quiriconi**, host of the *One Broken Mom* podcast, and
> author of *The Fearless Woman's Guide to Starting a Business*

"Gibson has written another powerful book that captures the reader's interest with her genuine concern that the reader has 'the best possible life.' Although she addresses those primarily affected by EI parents, friends, and families, this book has suggestions and insights that everyone can relate to and learn from. I myself read it two times as a retired therapist, and will certainly suggest it to other colleagues and friends."

>—**Judy K. Snider, MSW/ACSW**, coauthor of *I Love You,*
> *Be Careful*—a Mom's Choice Award winner

"You are worth it, you are enough, you are important, and you deserve to be loved no matter what you have felt in your relationship with your parents. With the guidance of this book, start the healing process by taking care of yourself so you can grow and gain confidence. The only relationship you will be in until the end of your life is the one you create with yourself."

—**Joanna Gutral,** psychologist at SWPS University in
Warsaw, Poland; certified cognitive behavioral psychotherapist;
psychoeducation leader; and podcaster at Kind Mind

"A gift to yourself all packaged into a beautifully written book. Lindsay Gibson gives you the skills, and sparks of insight you never knew you needed, to help you along on your journey toward living a happier, more fulfilling life."

—**Tara Bixby, LPC,** founder of courageously.u, and
host of *The Courageously.u Podcast*

"This book is essentially about love. Lindsay Gibson speaks directly to the reader with healing empathy and love, offering a guide for compassionate and healthy love of self and others. She shares her wisdom in short passages filled with empowering strategies for self-care and hilarious metaphors. Her gems of insights will evoke reactions from rollicking laughter to grief, but ultimately will inspire you with hope and courage."

—**Julia C. Smith, PhD,** licensed clinical psychologist

"Like a warm, gentle, and caring mother who sits us down regularly to teach us how to live a good life, Lindsay Gibson reparents us with this well-written, intelligible book. Self-care is one of the most difficult but rewarding of tasks for the survivor of EI parents, yet Gibson has managed to unfold every layer of it in a way that makes us understand and want to love ourselves."

—**Andrea Mathews,** therapist, speaker, and
author of *Letting Go of Good*

Self-Care *for* Adult Children *of* Emotionally Immature Parents

Honor Your Emotions,
Nurture Your Self &
Live with Confidence

LINDSAY C. GIBSON, PsyD

New Harbinger Publications, Inc.

Publisher's Note

This publication is designed to provide accurate and authoritative information in regard to the subject matter covered. It is sold with the understanding that the publisher is not engaged in rendering psychological, financial, legal, or other professional services. If expert assistance or counseling is needed, the services of a competent professional should be sought.

Distributed in Canada by Raincoast Books

NEW HARBINGER PUBLICATIONS is a registered trademark of New Harbinger Publications, Inc.

New Harbinger Publications is an employee-owned company.

Copyright © 2021 by Lindsay Gibson
New Harbinger Publications, Inc.
5720 Shattuck Avenue
Oakland, CA 94609
www.newharbinger.com

Cover design by Sara Christian; Interior design by Michele Waters-Kermes; Acquired by Tesilya Hanauer; Edited by Jennifer Holder

---

Library of Congress Cataloging-in-Publication Data

Names: Gibson, Lindsay C., author.
Title: Self-care for adult children of emotionally immature parents : honor your
    emotions, nurture your self, and live with confidence / Lindsay C. Gibson, PsyD.
Description: Oakland : New Harbinger Publications, 2021.
Identifiers: LCCN 2021013406 | ISBN 9781684039821 (trade paperback)
Subjects: LCSH: Self-confidence in adolescence. | Self-help techniques for teenagers.
    | Adult children of dysfunctional families--Mental health. | Emotional maturity. |
    Dysfunctional families--Psychological aspects.
Classification: LCC BF575.S39 G523 2021 | DDC 158.1--dc23
LC record available at https://lccn.loc.gov/2021013406

Printed in the United States of America

25   24   23

10   9   8   7   6   5   4

To my sister, Mary Carter Babcock,
who has always seen the best in me.

Contents

Part II: Dealing with People

Part III: Coping with Challenges

Introduction: Life Skills You Were Never Taught

This is a book to keep you company on your journey to self-discovery. Pick it up as a reminder to self-engage whenever you feel pressured to ignore your own well-being. If you had emotionally immature (EI) parents, you were probably expected to put them first. Nurturing and being true to yourself are not things that EI parents usually teach their children. Your parents' vulnerabilities and distortions, which I describe in my previous books, meant they couldn't show you how to sense and feel your way to a solution that is just right for you and the circumstances. So I compiled these short pieces of insight to help you remember what you need to feel whole, confident, and to have your best possible life.

This collection is designed to put you on a quest for self-awareness and fulfillment, to encourage certain attitudes and practices to make life easier and more enjoyable. I wrote these pieces to give you encouragement whenever you need it. The insights will tap that deep vein of authenticity that courses through you so you can be more yourself than ever before. I want you to feel you are back in touch with yourself, honoring your emotions, as you recall truths about yourself that may have been misplaced. There's no denying the thrill that comes when reading something that brings back a truth that had been lost from awareness. May you experience a spark of recognition as you read each piece, a click that says, "That's me" or "Yes, I knew that" even though you're reading it for the very first time.

These pieces on self-care, relationships, and how to approach problems will be the reminders you need to nurture your emerging self, to honor your inner world, and to protect yourself emotionally. In other words, they will encourage you to be true to yourself first.

In previous books, I have explained the phenomenon of emotional immaturity instructively, teaching and guiding in a linear fashion. But please read this collection of short pieces, meant to spark insight, with a looser approach. Read them as you are inspired to, for brief, hopefully enjoyable observations and reflections that aim to give you confidence in managing your greatest challenges. We'll also try out new ideas and different approaches to help move you into harmony with your *authentic self*. This inner self is where you find peace, happiness, and deep self-confidence. It makes you feel good about yourself, and you'll realize that life and its challenges have meaning and messages for your growth. These insight-pieces are grouped into sections on taking care of yourself, fostering relationship health, and confidently coping with life's challenges. These three areas are the gateways to a happier, more fulfilling life.

In the first section, we'll look at how self-care is built on self-awareness. As you become more skillfully self-aware and active on your own behalf, knowing what you really want, you will feel more competent and life will feel more manageable. You will be able to trust your inner world and protect yourself emotionally.

Next, we'll tackle the world of relationships and its challenges. We'll explore finding love and appreciating differences. We'll look at how to deal with difficult people, too. Interactions always go better when you know yourself and respond to others in such a way that you don't lose yourself. You don't have to give free passes for hurtful behavior or make excuses for other people's limitations. Instead, you can be realistic about them, admitting their effect on you, and stop making yourself responsible for their self-esteem and happiness. You alone get to decide how much time and attention you have to spare for difficult people.

Fortunately, there are also kind and helpful people in life as well who make you believe in yourself and feel emotionally safe. As you experience their positivity and unconditional acceptance, it nourishes your inner strength. These delightful people show you that good relationships are supposed to be about mutual enjoyment and encouragement instead of one person's enhancement at the cost of someone else's sacrifice. These special beings will point you toward love, trust, and honoring your feelings.

In the section about parenting, we'll look at which attitudes and approaches work best with children. Many people with EI parents fear they might become EI parents themselves and don't want to do to their children what was done to them. But if you are a self-reflective person who understands a handful of essential things about children and relating to people in general, you needn't worry. Once you understand your own past and how you were treated, you won't pass that on to anyone else, much less your own children. And once you grasp the bigger picture about what children are here to teach us, you will learn from them in ways that you never imagined.

When you grow up with EI parents, having a difference of opinion or setting a limit is labeled as selfish and uncaring. You are taught that nothing short of sacrificing yourself will ever prove loyalty and love, and that to think about yourself is the same thing as abandoning others. You may also be taught that ordinary life challenges are unjustified, unfair, and likely to overwhelm you. You are taught by example to be afraid of anything you cannot absolutely control. But there's another approach to life that we will explore, one in which you can take care of yourself and handle situations with acceptance and skill instead of panic.

In the last section of this book, you'll learn more productive approaches to life and how to cope with challenges. You'll see how life is showing you all the time how to accept its terms and deal well with it, if only you are willing to listen. You'll see how life keeps asking you to be active on your own behalf. With this approach to problems, you can see setbacks as calls to creativity and disappointments as prompts to consider anew what you truly want.

When you see life in such positive terms—not as senselessly inscrutable, but as meaningful and supportive to your growth—you begin to understand that stress can be treated as a warning signal that you are getting off track. You can heed stress's message by slowing down, tuning in, and trusting your ability to *sense* your way through a problem and work gently with your fears so you create effective solutions.

You are creating your life all the time. Will your life be a war against reality, a struggle against the facts like it is for many EI people? Or will you try to make things easier, to be more straightforward, to start from the ending you want, and work your way back to the beginning you're about to create? Will you be friendly with your mistakes and forbearing in those times when you can't see anything to be proud of in yourself? Those are the moments when life is asking you to be an artist, a really good one, who transcends mistakes and leaves spaces enough for creativity to breathe through the openings. You'll live your life more confidently and skillfully as soon as you start seeing it as your creation instead of something that is being done to you.

This book will activate new insights and build skills to make your life fuller and you more friendly toward yourself. Its goal is to attune you with your own authenticity and the wisdom of life. These insights will activate a search in you at a deeper level for the real you, a self-reflective process that will make change easier than you imagined.

If you've gotten out of synch with yourself, don't despair. If you've gotten tangled up in inherited issues from your parents, tiptoeing around their vulnerabilities by making yourself tentative and small, you can change that. If you've learned to judge yourself, you can quit it. None of these things has anything to do with the true nature of you. You were not made to be confused, guilty, or judged. The only sensible question in life is what you're going to do with what you've got.

The true nature of all life (including yours) is that it wants to go in the direction of expansion, thriving, and more life. But you may have learned to hold yourself back out of love, loyalty, and fear related to your childhood attachments. Others may have set conditions on what is necessary for you to be worthy, when actually you were worthy all along. Once you are more self-aware and back in touch with yourself, guilt and distortions just won't stick anymore. They will slide right off you because they no longer make sense once you are aligned with yourself, your life, and the right kind of people. You'll realize life is not out to hold you back and you are not selfish for being self-protective. You are not uncaring because you got tired, and nobody has the right to tell you what you should think and feel. These are mistaken beliefs that violate your basic rights and that you can drop as soon as you're ready.

The insights in this book will prepare you for that day when pleasing others is just a nice thing to do, freely embarked upon, and not a begging for the goodness that was yours anyway from the beginning. Here's to your new life, where you take good care of yourself like a proud, devoted, mature parent. Here's to your confidence that it is safe to be who you are. May you find relationships with kindred souls and look upon life as a challenging game that yields to your right approach. If these pieces of insight turn out to be your worthy companions in this process, no one will be happier than me.

PART I

Protecting and Caring for Yourself

Be True to Yourself

If you grew up putting others first too much, you may end up living a life of reaction rather than one of fulfillment. Instead, you can learn to become your own champion and protector, valuing and supporting who you are on the inside. The self-awareness you gain will center and ground you in your true self. Finding your authentic self is an enlivening process that keeps on giving once you resolve never to misplace it again.

1 Build a Better Relationship with Yourself

Be as available to yourself as you would be with someone you love.

Your relationship with yourself is the most vital relationship you have, essential for real connection with other people. Knowing yourself and appreciating what you find there make you become a fuller human being better capable of understanding and loving others. Unfortunately, you may neglect this inner relationship if you grew up in a family that discounted your inner world.

In childhood, when people invalidate or dismiss your inner experiences, your inner world seems unworthy of being taken seriously. If others won't listen to your deepest feelings, you start tuning out what goes on inside you. You learn to turn away from the rich inner world that could sustain you regardless of outer circumstances.

People who have disconnected from themselves discount their feelings by saying things like "I know this is stupid, but…" or "This is such a small thing; I'm embarrassed to admit it." Their attitude toward their inner experience is full of shame. Not trusting their inner guidance, they are sheepish about their real feelings. But your inner experience is who you are. It's your job to notice and understand what goes on inside you. To be emotionally healthy, you need to be as available to yourself as you would be with someone you love.

When you disregard your own feelings and thoughts, your inner world feels empty and you start obsessing over other people and external circumstances. You then try to get other people to fill the vacuum left behind by your own emotional self-neglect. This further disconnects you from your inner world, reinforcing the false belief that security and stimulation can only come from outside yourself. Relationships become frustrating under these conditions because you're looking to other people for a validation that is already yours.

No amount of social activity will fill the emptiness where there should be a robust relationship with yourself. When you judgmentally reject your true thoughts and feelings, you create a life of anxious dependency in which no power is greater than someone's opinion of you.

Take your inner experiences seriously. Process them fully. Give yourself adequate contemplative time. Put your thoughts down in a daily journal. Write down your dreams. Learn to become familiar with your inner world through meditation. By so doing, you show dedication to yourself as worthy of being listened to and honored.

It's the only way to build a strong inner self of your own. Watch and you will see how your inner world uses inspiration and intuition to nudge you toward happiness and well-being. Only by making a conscious, deliberate decision to honor your inner counsel can you get centered and self-directing. Once you start attending to your inner feedback, you know how things are really affecting you.

Your authentic self will always let you know when you have gotten too far away from who you really are. Start paying attention and listening to this inner guidance. It tracks your inner state, updating you through your emotions, energy levels, and unexpected thoughts. It constantly monitors whether you are happy or not. It shows what's best for you by raising or lowering your energy as you consider choices. As your thoughts and plans line up more with the needs of your true self, you will feel light, energized, and uplifted. When your interest surges and you feel focused and intent, you are probably onto something that is right for you. Start paying attention and listening to this inner guidance.

Conversely, if your energy sinks as you consider something, it's probably a poor match. A significant energy drop means there's little about the situation that feeds the real you. It would seem almost unnecessary to mention this, but it's astounding how often we feel our energy drop and yet proceed anyway because we tell ourselves it's the right thing to do. As most of us know, this usually turns out badly in the long run.

You have the ability to flourish and nurture yourself as a human being. You can't be good to others if you don't value yourself first. If you feel guilty and put yourself last, you may secretly expect others to take care of you because you aren't doing it for yourself. But don't give in to the pernicious idea that others should be more attentive to your needs than you are.

If you need more proof about the value of a good relationship with yourself, think about all the accomplished people who got that way by paying deep attention to their inner world. We grant that right to famous actors, Nobel scientists, great musicians, and world-renowned artists. Nobody ever questions if such people should be paying so much attention to their thoughts and inspirations or if it's okay for them to safeguard their time and energy from other people's demands. We should do no less for ourselves.

2　You Have the Right to Be Here

Injuries to self-esteem come from feeling that your uniqueness was rejected.

When someone mentions having low self-esteem, I think of that old cartoon with the man in the doctor's office complaining of a headache as he sits there with an arrow stuck through his head. The joke is that the headache is the least of his worries, and that is the same story with low self-esteem. People with poor self-esteem have a deeper problem than they think. Their deeper problem is that, somewhere along the way, someone has made them feel uncertain about whether they deserve to be here at all.

There are countless people walking around, holding jobs, and raising children who continue to question whether or not they are entitled to be here in the first place. They never quite have that rock-solid feeling that they belong and are valued. They may think their roles and jobs are worthwhile, but they are not so sure about the inner essence of themselves.

Yet all children come into this world with unquestioning self-acceptance of their needs, which is the root source of all self-esteem. A person with secure self-esteem knows the reality of his or her inner needs and knows that those needs are worthy of fulfillment. Doubting the legitimacy of these needs undermines the very foundation of one's self-worth.

People with low self-esteem come into my office wondering, *What's the matter with me?* But I think instead, "What *happened* to you?" I think this because I know these people did not enter the world feeling flawed or doubting their right to be here—that is, not until they encountered the bow and arrow of another person's rejection or criticism.

Ask yourself just who it was in your life that enjoyed archery so much. EI parents often carry quivers filled with debasing comments to shoot at you. Low self-esteem is exactly like going through life with a head full of their arrows. You cannot think without running into those internalized, sharp, piercing arrowheads.

Injuries to self-esteem come from feeling that your uniqueness was rejected. People with low self-esteem carry this story in their body language; they are constantly trying to make themselves appear absent.

Yet the longing for life and belonging is so strong that even arrow-shy people may one day question their low opinion of themselves. They wake up to their existential right to be here and to express what they need, finally overcoming their low self-esteem.

It is up to each and every one of us to sit ourselves down and accept that because we are here, we are supposed to be here. Once you have settled that question for yourself—and figured out who the archers were in your life—it is no longer just about improving self-esteem. It expands into the joys of self-expression and the right to self-protection. Self-esteem means you have decided you have the right to be here—and on top of that, to enjoy it too.

3   A Case of Mistaken Identity

Nobody finds it easy to be someone else.

I always notice it when a person in therapy says, "That's just not me" or, another favorite, "I'm not the kind of person who…" When people talk about themselves this way, I can hear the tinny echo of a distorted self-concept. Their denial just does not ring true.

Instead it sounds like a hand-me-down belief that the person took on about herself or himself, like something picked up at the flea-market of other people's opinions. What such individuals are rejecting is a trait or behavior that doesn't fit their overly narrow concept of themselves. Maybe that tinny off-note I heard was the sound of anxiety about stepping outside of their family's concept of them, imposed by EI parents.

A rigid or easily threatened parent will make it very clear that certain traits and behaviors are bad and deserve rejection or punishment. At the same time, such a parent may show warmth or approval if the child acts in ways that the parent can relate to.

When a child's nature is compatible with the parent's personality, there is harmony inside the child because the child fits nicely into the parents' expectations. The child feels secure being similar to Mom or Dad. Such identification allows for both connection and growth. But when children have to be something they are not in order to please the adults, especially EI parents, anxiety, shame, or depression soon follow. They start to feel like an imposter or feel they never do things well enough. That is because, at some level, the parent has given them the message they ought to be different than what they really are. These children must strain to fit in.

Naturally cooperative, malleable children—which fits the description of internalizer children of EI parents—will try hard to convince themselves that they must be wrong because the parent must be right. These children form an identity based on what they think they should be. Traits that don't fit are disowned.

Maybe this could work if it were not for the tremendous energy it takes to *not* be who you really are. The more you must please a parent, the less energy you have for mature self-development and finding your own path. Burying your true nature for the sake of family acceptance is both physically and emotionally exhausting.

Your ambitions, attractions, interests, and dreams tell you who you really are. They pull you toward the things that give you the best return on your efforts. Following them increases energy, optimism, and hopefulness because they are inherently empowering. They may cause anxiety if EI parents disapprove, but just remember that anxiety is often the by-product of growth. We all feel a little odd or scared when we try a new behavior.

So if you catch yourself saying, "I'm not that kind of person," ask yourself, "How do I know that?" Is it true deep in your soul, or is it because you were made to feel uncomfortable about those interests? Part of the fun of doing psychotherapy is watching people start to ask themselves these questions, as they open up to being different from how their families saw them. There is nothing like the joy that comes up when you discover that your inhibitions and self-limiting beliefs were just a case of mistaken identity.

4 Be Proud of Yourself

Pride is the natural sensation of delight in growth.

Nothing grows without delight. Green-thumbed gardeners know this, and so do parents who cherish their children. Showing delight in someone's growth gives the person fuel to keep trying. Good bosses do it, the best spouses do it, and we should do it too. Enthusiasm for our own progress is the most powerful motivator we have.

Praise from others can be as big as a whoop of joy or it can be as subtle as a softening of the eyes. But whatever form it takes, the person being praised feels proud he or she did it right. In childhood, praise guides the way, like a light along the path. There is no mystery to it; you just follow the smiles. Later on, you learn to give yourself that good feeling by feeling proud of yourself. Pride is the natural sensation of delight in growth.

But all too often, healthy pride gets confused with narcissism. If you are proud of yourself, you might fear you will be disliked or taken down a notch. As a result, some people superstitiously deny pleasure in their accomplishments in order to ward off a comeuppance. Pride has even been labeled a sin, and acting conceited is a social no-no.

Another practice that has given healthy pride a bad name is excessive praise for the smallest childhood success, from earning tokens in the classroom to the trophy glut at Little League. Many adults are turned off by this overpraise, sensing that the children are being done no favor. In fact, research has shown that many children overpraised for success end up becoming more cautious and less motivated than the kids who were praised only for their amount of effort, successful or not.

However, if you as an adult are trying to make positive changes in your life, then you must notice and take time to feel good about even your smallest successes. To do so is just as important as figuring out what you wanted to change in the first place. You encourage yourself to grow, taking pleasure in your progress. The pleasure you feel tells the brain to keep strengthening these new tracks of changed behavior.

Unfortunately, instead of noticing and celebrating your positive changes, you might tell yourself not to get a swelled head. Even worse, you may tell yourself that because you feel so good, something bad might happen, just to even things out. The brain then puts the brakes on that new outlook or behavior because your mind senses anxiety, not pleasure.

Instead of dashing past your best moments, just when things are changing for the better, you ought to be asking yourself how you did it. If you don't analyze and take pride in what you did right, you will not know how to get there again, nor will you have the enthusiasm to keep trying. Analyzing how you got to a better place makes it more than a happy accident; you become conscious of a skill that you can hone further.

Deliberately pausing to feel delight encourages more growth. But many people find it hard to feel proud of themselves for very long. They squirm and resist, minimizing the fact that their changes had a huge impact for the better. Many times, people do not think it's possible to really change, and they ignore the evidence of it as soon as they do it. Embarrassed to praise themselves, they undo their delight and accomplishment, insisting they are the same old people—which is exactly the way to guarantee they will stay the same old people.

If you want to keep having good feelings and a better life, notice what you did right and make a point to feel good about each accomplishment. You are not being prideful or vain; you are learning to feel proud of yourself for well-earned success. That warm glow in your chest and broadened sense of possibility are the natural, organic results of getting it right. If you make a point to pause and enjoy the moment, you can fan that spark into a sustaining fire of motivation. If you snuff it out too quickly, you extinguish not just the good feeling of the moment but your energy for the future. Take every chance you can to feel good about feeling good. Learn to enjoy the sensation of pride. It is what successful people have always done to keep their motivation strong. You won't be an egoist; you will be an enthusiast—a self-enthusiast. Then you can pass it along to others.

5   Listening to Your Soul

When you are attuned with your soul, you feel right with the world.

As a psychologist, I usually use a psychological term like *true self* instead of *soul* to refer to the deepest part of a person. But sometimes *soul* is the only word to use. When referencing our deepest needs and motives, *soul* is the term that fits. It's a beautiful, poetic concept that can capture our internal experience like none other.

Soul is shorthand for the *you of you*. It is the unifying source of your inner world and, as such, connotes the deepest center of your being. Calling this personal nucleus the *self* can sound too cerebral or rationalistic, as if it could be known and controlled. But the word *soul* has a deeper, grander quality, like something more mysterious and ancient, something with a powerful agenda of its own. Listening to my self is not as profound as what my soul might say to me.

Although *psychology* literally means the study of the soul, somewhere along the way, psychologists decided that the soul wasn't scientific enough. In order to make psychology a real science, the soul had to go. Psychologists gave up their intimacy with the soul and instead let religion become its brand holder. Psychology turned to behavior, research, testing, defense mechanisms, and anything to do with the mind. Anything beyond that—like the purpose of life or spiritual issues—became off-limits.

In the beginning, the young science of psychology was just trying to make a name for itself, but it drove an unnecessary wedge between the spiritual and the psychological. That was unfortunate because understanding the soul is something that both religion and science could contribute to. Psychology wouldn't be hurt by a little spiritual mystery, and religion could stand a bit of science. Neither side of this human experience needs to reject the other.

When you talk about your soul, you are accepting that you have a crucial, mysterious part of yourself that is completely interior, often subconscious, somehow sacred, and deserving of respect and reverence. This internal center also knows what is deeply right or wrong for you. It can even cause moral injury when you go against it. It seems to know what you're here for and whether or not you are fulfilling your purpose.

If you talk yourself out of your dreams or into settling for less, your soul is unhappy and lets you know it with agitation and yearning. You might even experience anxiety or depression, signs that you have become separated from your innermost being and no longer feel whole. This is often the result of trying to be something that you are not, such as trying to fit in with or please an EI person. But when you are attuned with your soul, the meaning of life feels self-evident, and you feel right with the world.

You must take the soul seriously for your own psychological health. If you believe your thinking mind alone can guide you on the deepest questions of existence, you soon end up in a confusion of competing motives. Only the inner wisdom of the soul urges you toward meaningful pursuits and true self-actualization. People who pay attention to their soul's promptings find meaning and connection more easily. As they trust their soul, they are guided to fulfilling experiences.

By the way, listening to your soul is not being selfish. "Selfish" is such a common accusation from an EI parent that you may accuse yourself of it often. But know this: You also give to others when you are a calm yet vibrant person who is pursuing meaningful interests. It's the people who don't listen to their soul and don't feel that self-connection who end up causing the most suffering for others.

I have decided that I don't have to know where the soul comes from. I just have to acknowledge that there is something inside that energizes and guides us. Perhaps we have done our soul a disservice to quibble over whose ideological house it should live in. Maybe it's not necessary for the soul to be pulled between ideologies, like a child in a disputed custody case. Perhaps the idea of soul could exist apart from either religion or psychology, in its own category of undeniable inner human experience. Maybe that's all you need to know in order to use it for your good and the good of the world. When you get whole with your soul, life goes well.

Openness, purpose, fulfillment, and a sense of connection with something larger are just some of the benefits of respecting the soul. You don't have to believe in God to believe in your soul. Believing in God is just one of the ways you can take the soul seriously.

Practice Emotional Self-Protection

Sometimes it is not enough just to have respect for yourself. Sometimes you have to actively protect yourself from people and situations that would drain your energies or hurt your feelings. Looking out for yourself is a primary responsibility, whether it's setting boundaries or making sure that others aren't allowed to limit your life.

6   Loosening the Ties That Bind

DNA is not a life sentence.

People have devised many different ways of getting into and out of relationship agreements. We get into a marriage with a marriage license and out of it with a divorce decree. We start business partnerships with contracts and end debts with payoff certificates. For most relationships, we like to know where they begin and when they stop.

One type of relationship is not regulated so clearly, and that is the relationship between adult children and their parents. The law defines the obligations of parents toward their minor children. We also informally acknowledge a parent's right to disown or disinherit an adult child of any age. However, we have no words for it when an adult child wishes to end contact with a parent. There's no ceremony, no legal document, nothing to mark the event.

Many people avoid problems with their parents by simply moving away. But there are other situations where the relationship with EI parents becomes truly problematic because these parents insist on their right to time with their adult child, whether the child wants it or not. This type of parent is often emotionally immature and incapable of the kind of empathy that is necessary for respectful relationships.

EI parents can't seem to imagine the feelings of their adult children. They resist your attempts to set boundaries in the relationship. Such parents use guilt to force a closeness that you may not want, and your requests for more space and respectful treatment seem to fall on deaf ears. Self-preoccupied parents act as if they are entitled to your life, as well as their own, and seem baffled and offended when you balk at this. All kinds of boundary violations can ensue, from intruding upon your personal life to pushing opinions when none are asked. Parents who enter without knocking, tell you what you're doing wrong, or insist on giving unwanted gifts are examples of this sense of morbid entitlement.

You may not recognize these annoying behaviors as disrespectful boundary violations and instead feel guilty for wanting to avoid your parents. Some adult children have been so strictly conditioned to believe their parents are well-meaning—just wanting the best for them—that they think they themselves must be the ones with the problem. In these cases, the person ends up feeling anxious or guilty because he or she feels bad about "blaming" the parent for anything.

If confronted, EI parents will discount your distress by claiming there is no reason to be upset with them. Such parents see themselves as interested, loving, and only trying to help. But the fist in this velvet glove is the parents' ironclad feeling that you still belong to them, as if you were an extension of the parents. EI parents try to control you with critical comments about anything that does not put the parents' feelings first.

Many adult children do speak up clearly to these parents, only to find that the parents keep doing the same thing anyway. As the adult child, you then feel mystified and helpless. Setting limits is supposed to work, isn't it? What are you doing wrong that causes your EI parent to keep ignoring your requests? The answer is that modern communication skills are no match for someone who does not want to hear the word *no.*

Some parents mock their adult child's request for boundaries as ridiculously formal or as psychobabble. They can only see you in a satellite role, orbiting their much more important needs. If this parental expectation is not met, expect hurt, complaint, and, soon, anger.

After setting a limit, you usually feel you have made things worse. The attempt to communicate honestly about the relationship has led to hurt feelings and criticism, not cooperation. The parents' mood now radiates woundedness and blame, not at all what you had intended. You feel punished for protecting yourself and selfish for causing the parents' distress.

Sometimes with an especially stubborn parent, you have no choice but to withdraw from the relationship. You may have to set limits with the parent, up to and including no contact. The parent can be welcome to approach and reconcile, but the requested boundaries need to be observed for the relationship to go forward. If an EI parent cannot respect this, you may need to break off contact again.

Sometimes people will feel guilty that they are not honoring their father or mother without thinking about what this really means. If you read that biblical commandment carefully, it does not say that you must love your father and mother, nor does it say you have to hang out with them. It certainly does not say that you should never respectfully say no to them. It just means that you should treat them with the respect than an older person deserves. It also suggests that we could honor them by making something good of ourselves. It is interesting that the people who feel most guilty about this issue are usually the ones who have been paragons of forbearance with their misbehaving parents.

DNA is not a life sentence. Your parents' biological gift of life may have brought you here, but you do not belong to your parents for the rest of your life. We all get to grow up and leave home. If your parents are not willing to play nice, you don't have to spend time with them. You can always honor them from a distance.

7   The Purpose of Boundaries

Voicing boundaries is just a way of saying who you are and what you prefer.

Emotionally sensitive and empathic people who were raised by an EI parent can find it hard to set boundaries. Caring about other people's feelings often leads to feeling guilty for establishing limits. You might worry that saying no will make you appear unkind, selfish, or even rejecting. You don't want anyone to feel bad.

Maybe part of the problem is that we use hard phrases like *establishing boundaries* and *setting limits,* which sound like we are stiff-arming other people away with no empathy at all. But limit-setting doesn't have to be harsh or controlling; it can just be a positive way of *creating space* for yourself. Think of it as making room for *you,* not aggressing against others. Voicing boundaries is just a way of stating your preferences. It's nothing more than being honest about what makes you feel comfortable and safe.

Unfortunately, dominant people, such as many EI parents, often become resentful and pushy when you don't do as they like. They act as if respecting your comfort level is somehow robbing them of theirs. They may see your boundary as a challenge to their right to have what they want. Essentially, they accuse you of being unfair for objecting to their intrusions. While this coercive behavior is easy to spot in hindsight, in the moment it might catch you off guard because you hate to give offense or make others upset with you. That's why it's so important to see boundaries as simply preserving your personal space and freedom of choice. You're not being mean for stating your own preferences. You don't have to be so empathic to them that you forget about how *you* feel.

In the past, assertiveness techniques emphasized standing up to others in a way that was tough, stubborn, insistent, and defensive. But all that wasn't actually necessary. When other people push too hard, all you have to do is stay true to yourself and keep restating your preferences. Emotional bullies don't have the right to tell you what you should be comfortable with.

Communicating your limits is especially important in the early stages of a relationship because you get to see what happens when you don't go along with what the other person wants. In her *One Broken Mom* podcast, host Ameé Quiriconi explains that introducing small boundaries early in a relationship is a great way of finding out whether this new person will respect your individuality or try to control you. Expressing preferences and asking for space are emotionally intimate communications. A good relationship candidate will enjoy hearing about your limits as a way of learning more about you. In fact, your honesty will be appreciated. Stating a boundary makes you a little bit vulnerable and is therefore a relational gift; you are telling the person you like them enough to be genuine with them. Someone who *wants* to get to know you will appreciate this.

Safe people have no desire to overstep your bounds; they *want* to know how you feel. When you ask for space, thoughtful people may show curiosity or compassion, but they won't react with pressure, arguments, or counteroffers. To a considerate person, everyone has the right to say no. But to egocentric people, no one has the right to turn them down.

Asking for space or declining an offer is not aggression. If someone is offended by a legitimate boundary, that's the kind of exaggerated reaction that is a red flag of emotional immaturity. Don't imagine their hurt feelings to be more significant than they really are. You are merely communicating what you need to feel your best. No decent person will make you feel bad for needing to feel good.

8 Why You're Emotionally Fatigued

Emotional fatigue is physically real.

Have you ever had an emotional encounter that left you limp with exhaustion? Then you know the special kind of fatigue that comes from *emotional work.* You can feel more drained after certain emotional experiences than if you had run a marathon. Physical effort is tiring of course, but emotional effort feels like somebody has zapped your very life force. This kind of fatigue is beyond what you can feel with muscles alone. It is telling you that your brain has been in hyperdrive, consuming glucose voraciously and sending blood flow to very energy-intensive parts of the brain. You have just had a neurological workout.

Emotionally sensitive people, like internalizer children of EI parents, are especially likely to get tired out by others' needs. If you are this way, you respond to bids for sympathy and attention because you are so empathic. The acute perceptiveness that sparks your sensitivity means that you will notice the smallest disharmonies in other people. And once you notice even a tiny bit of distress, your brain's *mirror neurons* will start firing away, subjecting you to an empathic workout that takes on a life of its own until you get away from the person. Your nerves are actually being overworked by involuntarily mirroring their discomfort as you wrack your brain over how to make things better for them.

In the old days of psychology, emotional symptoms were tied to the nervous system more directly. We used to talk about *nervous exhaustion, neurasthenia, neurosis,* and *nervous breakdowns.* These old terms were, in some ways, more fitting because they recognized the connection between our distress and our actual physical nervous system. They recognized that people were feeling bad because their nervous systems were overworked. Now we have shifted to *emotional disorders* and *psychopathology,* but I like the old terms because they tied emotional symptoms to the body itself. But how can just using your nervous system make you so tired?

One of the most interesting things about your nervous system is that it is responsible not just for doing but also for *not* doing. There are two kinds of processes the nervous system performs: initiating action and inhibiting action. Whenever you restrain yourself from the urge to act, you are doing as much work—often more—as if you had actually said or done something. The expression "biting my tongue" is a good metaphor to illustrate how one part of the nervous system clamps down to stop the action of another part. And this takes energy.

People who leap into action look like they are expending lots of energy. But people who pause, think, and problem solve (instead of popping off) are expending even more energy. This means that people who are empathic, self-reflective, and concerned about helping others are constantly draining their neurological batteries with their internal efforts. If this is you, your energy expenditure is not obvious because you are not showing any outward physical action. But on the inside, you are wrestling emotions, controlling reactions, considering future outcomes, and trying to find not just any solution but the best solution. This actually uses more energy than being reactive and impulsive.

Good parenting and good relationships demand complex neurological inhibitions, which require more effort than just blindly reacting. For instance, reacting punitively toward a defiant teenager takes less neurological energy—in the short run—than listening to the teen, calming him, and getting him to work with you rather than against you. The restrained approach gets you a better outcome in the long run, but in order to do it, you have also paid the price of activating some pretty energy-expensive real estate in multiple locations of your brain. Peacekeepers work hard on the inside, using brain systems that troublemakers don't even know are there.

Thank goodness for people who exert their brains to calm others and find constructive outcomes, whether it is dealing with a child or with global politics. This high level of mature behavior is a strenuous physical workout of the nerves and neurons, working brains double-time to find the optimal blend of both inhibition and action.

So now you know that the peculiarly exhausted sensation of emotional fatigue is physically real and coming from your actual nervous system. If you recognize this as genuine tiredness, you may be more willing to honor your needs for downtime after making those Herculean emotional efforts.

The whole neurological system does not need to cut off after mental exertion; it just needs to shift focus. The nervous system never stops being active—even in sleep, we breathe and dream—but after exertion, it wants to shift into other states, which relaxes the brain. That is why it is so crucial for caretakers and those who have to deal with difficult, dominating people such as EI parents to get away and engage in other replenishing activities and diversions. The tired brain wants to slip into a mode in which there is no need to watch your step, think of others, or inhibit thoughts and impulses. That is why laughing at a TV show or being with good friends is so relaxing. Your brain can just let go and no longer has to work at putting the brakes on itself. Free, unopposed mental functioning is relaxing and energizing.

If you ever find yourself saying, "Why am I so tired? I haven't been doing anything," stop and reconsider. Yes, you have been doing something. It was all those things you didn't say, all those destructive urges you didn't follow. That was a full day's work from your brain's point of view. From all the rest of us who benefited from your efforts and never knew it, thank you for all the work you did that we never even saw.

9 Healing from Emotional Injuries

An emotional injury reacquaints you with your heart if you're willing to let it.

Before we can heal an emotional injury, we first have to accept it. Too often, we reject our emotional injuries and hurt feelings as if they were needless interruptions—unwanted, beside the point, and interfering with our progress. It's understandable that you might want to hurry past them to get on with your life. But what if your hurt feelings are crucial to your maturation? What if they are important building blocks for your unique development?

What you are hurt by defines your individuality. Tolstoy said that happy families are all alike, but every unhappy family is unhappy in its own way. The same is true of us as individuals. The ways in which your emotional injuries affect you are unique to you.

Emotional injuries also soften up that hardened part of us that wants above all to be special and in command. This egoistic part lives in fear of anything or anyone that doesn't serve its shortsighted goals of pleasure and control. It sees life as exclusively about power, possession, and protection. It blames and judges everything and everybody, guarding its entitlements by keeping everyone at a distance. Sometimes it takes an emotional injury to get through its defenses.

Emotional injuries—such as hurt feelings, betrayals, and losses—reveal what truly matters to you. An emotional injury reacquaints you with your heart if you're willing to let it. Emotional pain drops you down into your deeper nature and into more genuine relationships with others. If allowed, your emotional injuries will open you into a more meaningful and deeper experience of life than the control-obsessed ego could ever imagine.

Any kind of healing process, physical or emotional, is governed by nature. Nature takes injury seriously—whether you're an animal, human, plant, or tree—and it applies energy and resources to make sure every weak place is made strong again. For instance, a tree lays down extra whorls of bark around injury sites, expending costly growth on strengthening repairs. In human terms, we repair emotional injuries with mental processing, experiencing our feelings, and honoring our vulnerability in the moment. We also heal ourselves emotionally with words by talking it out with someone. Our obsessive thinking and need to talk are like the swelling and inflammation that follow an injury; it may look like it's making things worse, but the body and mind want a thorough healing, not a quick fix. Nature takes its time in rebuilding our bark.

Unfortunately, our control-obsessed ego thinks that spending time to process emotional injuries is almost pathological. Many times, people with emotional injuries are encouraged to shake it off and move on. It's as if we have a morbid fear of getting stuck in emotional pain and never getting out. We do the same with loss and grieving, feeling pressure to quickly return to life as normal. After all, who wants to experience grief? But the deeper question is, who wants to be incapable of grief?

The key to successful emotional healing is to accept that you probably won't be the same afterward. The more you fight against this truth, the longer you may take to heal. You're better off accepting that emotional healing usually leaves some scars. Healing is not like a magic eraser—the goal shouldn't be to act like it never happened to you.

We may not need to look for meaning in a broken bone or cut finger, but broken hearts and crushing disappointments ask us to understand our pain and find meaning in the experience. That's a tall order when the injury is deep, but it seems to be our uniquely human way of healing. I think of emotional injuries as initially unwelcome guests who over time teach us a lot about ourselves. Our challenge is to find a way to have a good relationship with them even though they have caused us pain.

Emotional healing can take a long time, and even then, it won't be like it never happened. You'll be changed by it. But it's totally up to you to decide if you will be changed for the better. It's an enormous act of maturity to be willing to feel the hurt and integrate it into your life instead of railing against it. The challenge is to find meaning in your healing process. You do this by making it a conscious, deliberate focus of your life, giving it the time and thought necessary to slowly build up patches of wisdom and compassion around all the hurt places. Just like the tree, there can actually be more to you after an emotional injury, but only if you take your healing seriously.

10 Debug Your Mind

Any thought that makes you feel bad or hopeless is probably some form of malware.

Calling the brain a computer is a popular metaphor for this miraculous organ. And like a computer, your brain is highly vulnerable to invasive programs that are bad for its operating system. In the computer world, these destructive programs are collectively known as *malware* but individually might be called *viruses, bugs, Trojan horses,* or *worms.* Some of them are *drive-by downloads* that can cause *zombie computers.* Whether the goal is a complete takeover of your computer or just messing with some files, these malicious codes are installed by programmers who have gained remote and unauthorized access.

If you are a computer novice, you might not notice the presence of a bug until your computer starts acting up. If you took it to a specialist, though, they would detect the virus and start debugging your system. When it comes to mental viruses, you can do the same. You just have to know how.

Mental malware can get into our brains at any age, as long as the programmer is charismatic or powerful enough. But most influential malware starts in childhood, when we are socialized to believe all kinds of things that make life easier for the adults in our lives, especially EI parents. Because these socialization viruses often are based on expediency and not on any real logic, they can be a confusing hodgepodge of contradictory messages. When these contradictory rules kick in simultaneously, we are paralyzed between two equally insistent thoughts.

The first step in debugging your mental computer is to realize that this bug was probably installed before you were old enough to know the difference. Undoubtedly, you were given the message that it was for your own good. But as a rule of thumb, any thought that makes you feel bad or hopeless is probably some form of malware. Legitimate guilt and remorse tend to be fast-acting prompts that move us to corrective action. When we have actually done something wrong, we feel a strong, healthy urge to remedy it. On the other hand, mental malware just makes you feel like a failed person.

Early childhood malware likes to tell us that certain thoughts and feelings are bad. It makes us feel ashamed of our true reactions and confused about our motives. And of course, the malware will never disclose its control tactics. Instead you will be run by an invisible download installed in childhood that pretends to be your conscience. It makes you waste copious amounts of time and mental energy, trying to get yourself to think the right way and feeling bad when you fail. You become the perfect host for a virus that says you can never be good enough.

A good way to catch these viruses is to write down any thoughts that give you a bad feeling about yourself. As you record them over a day, you will get a good idea of how far this computer worm has spread in your thinking. Remember, brain malware is characterized by contradictory messages, mutually exclusive values, and absolute commandments that are full of exceptions. You can't succeed if you use mental malware to think with.

After you spot the virus's effect, the next step is to identify its source code. That would be the one-sentence draconian rule that your guilt or low self-esteem is based on. It might be that people must always love their families or that parents are always strong and right. It might tell you something like self-interest is bad, but success is good. (Just try to make that combination work.) You will see that these sweeping statements do not hold water or even make sense.

Next, your job is to expose the virus' code, deprogram it, and send the Trojan horse packing. You do this by contemplating each thought that makes you feel bad until you can spot its illogic and where it likely came from. Question it, disagree with it, and argue against it like a lawyer's cross-examination. Little by little, you can loosen the hold it has on you. Once you realize you have been unwittingly programmed, you can coolly observe its noxious effect and say an inner *no* every time it starts to make you feel bad.

To reprogram yourself, you then choose empowering adult beliefs that make sense in the grown-up world. It helps to make a two-columned list, writing down your old and new beliefs across from each other. You will see that you can't follow both, because they can't both be true. Then, when you're ready to give it up, literally cross out the previous virus-infected belief. Your EI parent did not know their pass-along virus was going to cause you so much trouble, and to let it linger in your brain is the worst kind of self-sabotage. A Trojan horse can look like a gift from the gods, but that sinking feeling will tell you that it's time to close the city gates.

Honor Your Inner World

Self-care begins with self-knowledge. You have an inner world that is constantly trying to guide you toward a happier, more fulfilling life if only you will listen to it. But in childhood you may have learned to disregard your inner messages and do what other people thought was right for you. There's a huge cost for that later, setting you up for living a life that is not what you want. Instead, try to rediscover yourself from the inside out, listening for those cues that tell you what to seek and what to avoid.

11 Pick Your Right Inner Voice

Your wise inner voice speaks with quiet certainty, while the voices of society, ego, and your EI parent are always pushing some agenda.

Nobody likes to admit he or she hears voices. People who mention something a voice told them in their head quickly add they did not mean *that* kind of voice. But of course most of us hear "voices," all the time, right here in our own minds. In fact, our inner conversations keep us sane. The thoughts of most normal people naturally take an inner verbal form, spoken to the self as a way of thinking things through.

What fascinates me is how we decide which of these inner voices to listen to. How do we tell which voice is a good source of guidance and which is going to get us into trouble? Many people have told me that they had a quiet knowing about a situation way before they took action on it. They could remember when a still, small voice told them the truth, even if they were not ready to accept what it had to say. Have you had this experience? Even years later, you recall that you knew all along that something was a bad idea. Yet instead, you followed the insistent voice telling you that you *must* do otherwise, regardless of how you felt or what you knew.

Your wise inner voice speaks with quiet certainty, while the voices of society, ego, and your EI parent are always pushing some agenda. Later, you might rue the fact that your still small voice was so quiet. "Why didn't it shout at me to stop?" you might ask, "Why didn't it make me get out?" Why is our essential voice so quiet and why does it take up so little room in our lives?

Originally, this voice was anything but still and small. Ask any parent of a two-year-old. Most of us start out with definite knowledge of what we like and do not like, where we want to go, and whom we want to be with. Back then, we could tell when people were hurting us, and we tried to avoid things that didn't feel good.

Our original inner guidance was as loud and penetrating as a foghorn, warning us off the rocks. But we were taught to mistrust this inner guide when it conflicted with the desires of others on whom we depended—especially our parents. Each time we mistrusted it, it grew smaller and dimmer, but it never went away.

As our true inner voice shrank, a strident, pushy voice shoved its way into top place. This voice emphasizes feelings of guilt and shame that originally were encouraged by EI parents and authority figures in order to make us compliant. This ego voice speaks insistently, using words like "should," "must," and "have to." It is the voice of compulsion. It makes us resentful, even as we give up control of our lives to others. The ego voice has an unrealistically urgent quality, often pushing us into situations while our other little voice keeps whispering to us, "This is not good for you."

The loud, insistent ego voice pushes and tires you, never letting up on what you should be doing next. Listening to it makes you feel stressed. ("There is so much to do! I should try harder! This is what it takes to be a good person!") You rarely notice that the voice is never satisfied, and it commands more and more from you every time you try to please it. Although you are assured that following it will somehow make you a better person, usually, you just feel worse.

The other voice, your natural voice of preference and self-preservation, is not compulsive and does give you a choice. It becomes insistent only in the most extreme situations of urgent danger. Short of that, it is content to tap gently on your consciousness as soon as you feel uncomfortable or unsafe. It is as though it *wants* you to have a choice, as though it is perfectly willing to let you make your mistakes and learn from them. It never says, "I told you so," because it doesn't want you to feel bad. It's just happy when you finally listen.

It should be easy to see which voice has your true best interests at heart. The loud, adamant ego voice wants you to *obey*. The still, small voice wants you to *think*. "Take all the time you need," it seems to say, "I want you to feel sure about this." The ego voice says the opposite: "Hurry up! Who cares how you feel? I'll tell you what's right!"

These voices offer very different styles of guidance. Which kind of advisor would you trust in real life? That is the one to trust inside your own head.

12 What Emotions Are For

Emotions show us when things are not good for us.

You have no choice about whether you are going to have a feeling or not. For a long time, there has been a popular belief in psychotherapy that feelings always require a preceding thought. Find the thought and fix the feeling; think a different thought and feel better. Yet this is so obviously incorrect, I am surprised it ever caught on. Often your emotions are caused by thoughts, but not always. You can certainly have emotions without thinking, thanks to millennia of instinctual evolution. You don't need thoughts, words, or concepts to experience an instinctual emotional reaction.

A person yelling, a look of disgust, a radiant face of joy—all trigger mirror neurons in your brain making you feel the other person's emotional state. This has nothing to do with whether you are thinking negative thoughts or letting them get to you. Their behavior goes directly to the emotional centers in your brain, intended or not. Going back to the origins of humankind, our emotional reactions to other people's expressions are our oldest form of interaction, predating language. All people in all cultures use the same basic emotional facial expressions, universal messages that are instantly readable. They reveal other people's emotional states and their intentions toward us. As a human, you will pick up emotional meanings at subtle levels, whether you intend to or not. As human beings evolved, the biggest threat to humans was other humans. The ability to quickly size up the intentions of a stranger might have made the difference between life and death. Trade with other groups also became possible because people could tell through gut feelings whether a stranger was likely to be trustworthy or not.

But in modern times, the mind has gotten out of hand. It now sets goals without consulting the emotions at all. Whoever gets you to accept an idea—especially when it goes against your deeper feelings—owns your soul. This has been the goal of brainwashers for centuries, and EI parents do it too. Once you've been trained to trust your thoughts over your feelings, you can be made to believe that bad situations and exploitative people are necessary in your life and even good for you.

Think of emotions as canaries in the coal mine. Your feelings indicate when conditions are not good for you. They show danger much faster than conscious thought. Emotions have one purpose in your life: to make you pay attention to vital information about your situation. If you don't listen to them, they will raise the volume. Much of psychotherapy is learning how to respect those messages.

But you don't always need psychotherapy to feel better. A willingness to explore your feelings in self-reflection or writing can help you decipher those messages, and confiding in a trusted friend can bring out your emotional truth in healing ways. Your emotions are not silly, pointless, or trying to upset you for no good reason. They are your sentinels. They exist only for your well-being and wholeness, and they will save you once you're willing to listen to their guidance.

13 Why You Feel Dread

Sometimes the point of a problem is to walk away from it, not solve it.

Dread is the true south of our emotional compass, more reliable in its guidance than almost any other feeling. We all know dread, that sinking, awful feeling when you cannot make yourself go forward. Just picture a dog on his ride to the vet: that's what dread looks like.

There is nothing like a pang of dread to let you know you are headed in the wrong direction. When it hits, it is impossible to talk yourself out of it. Rationalize all you want, but you will still dread the thing that is not good for your soul.

The trouble is that authority figures—EI parents especially—often teach you to discount and mistrust your sound, healthy dread reactions. If you dreaded school, you were told it was good for you. If you dreaded a task, you were informed it would make you a better person. Now, as an adult, if you dread doing something, you might tell yourself you are being weak. These are echoes of parental emotional coercion that didn't allow you to figure out what was causing your dread in the first place. EI parents effectively said that your instinctual reactions were illegitimate until approved by others.

When I think back on my own dread experiences, I have to say that in one way or another, I was 100 percent right about there being something majorly wrong with the situation for me. Almost without fail, some part of myself could always tell upfront that this thing was going to cost me.

If I were working with you on your personal growth issues, getting you to trust your dread would be a major step forward. Due to early conditioning, you may have become confused instead of confident about your instincts to avoid certain situations, people, and things. It seems unacceptable to cope with things by avoiding them, doesn't it? You were probably encouraged to charge ahead and confront things in order to change them. If you have the urge to avoid something or someone that you dread, you might feel guilty, even cowardly. You are supposed to face your problems and overcome them, right?

Well, that depends on what your goal is. The fact is that not all problems can be fixed. Sometimes, the point of a problem is to walk away from it, not solve it. I'll give an example. One of my clients had an overbearing mother who would regularly berate her about her choices in life. No amount of explanation, limit setting, or confrontation stopped this mom from pushing her toxic opinions. Needless to say, my client *dreaded* phone calls from this woman. One day she realized that she did not have to talk to her mother at all—and if she did, she could avoid or sidestep any topic that brought out the worst in Mom. This was not a sign of this person's weakness. It was a mark of her sheer good sense.

In some situations, avoidance makes sense, and dread tells us when such avoidance is needed. Dread can tell you when you are about to beat your head against a brick wall. It can tell you that you are about to do something that is going to cost you dearly yet give you little in return.

One of the most interesting things to me is when one of your previously sought-after goals or activities begins to be dreaded. Your heart is no longer in it, and the thought of continuing to do it leaves you feeling exhausted. Whatever rewards there used to be have lost their appeal and your instinct is to withdraw from the situation. This is because your motivation to keep doing things the same old way is gone. You can no longer spin yourself "up" enough to play the part. Sometimes when you have become too alienated from your real self's needs, dread is the only thing that can still get your attention.

If you pay attention to each of your dread experiences and heed their warnings, they will not accumulate into feelings of depression. When dread occurs, it means you still know what it is you do *not* want to do. This is how successful, happy people stay that way. They instinctively avoid things that deplete their energy so they can have motivation for the things that matter to them. Dread won't let you be mean to yourself. Listen to what it is telling you, and you'll be setting a course toward happiness and growth.

14 Don't Be Undermined into Depression

A little unwanted advice is all it takes to make your energy drop.

All people have to do to bring you down is follow a simple three-part recipe: (1) listen to your ideas or desires, then offer helpful criticism; (2) push you to accept their much better idea; and (3) when you protest and get upset, tell you to calm down and explain in a slow, rational voice why their way makes much more sense.

This will work especially well if they can convince you that their better idea will save money, time, and inconvenience. If they keep this up whenever you have a good idea, you will begin to have trouble making up your mind, followed by a mysterious loss of initiative. Over time, you will start to show signs of classic depression: low energy, hopelessness, poor self-esteem, self-doubt, feelings of worthlessness, sadness, and trouble sleeping. At this point, you'll be ready to see a mental health professional who will diagnose you with depression. It is so easy!

People who are homemakers or stay-at-home parents are especially vulnerable to this kind of depression. For instance, we would have no trouble understanding a career employee's becoming depressed following the loss of his job, title, or daily routine. It would be no mystery to us why the poor guy was down in the dumps over being thwarted in his quest for personal prestige and satisfaction. It's a simple equation. We get it.

However, the lead-up to stay-at-home people's depression is often a slow accumulation of frustrations that we do not see happening. The events contributing to their emotional downfall are frequently so small and commonplace that we overlook them as causes at all. The ones that do catch our attention—a loss, a marital problem, a difficult child—are likely to be just the last straw in a long series of personal frustrations. People are able to put up with a lot, but there comes the point where it catches up with them.

One depressed woman I knew began to feel better when she stopped letting her husband make "innocent" changes to her plans and choices. For years, whenever she came up with an idea for something she wanted to do, her husband would show her why her way was inefficient and offer her a more sensible alternative. She was systematically being deprived of her own autonomy in choosing what she wanted to do.

If you had a controlling EI parent, you might be accustomed to people puncturing your initiative. It is very subtle but very deflating. A little unwanted advice is all it takes to create a sudden drop in interest and energy. There is no satisfaction or fulfillment in carrying out someone else's version of your own idea.

Many employed people would instantly grasp this concept if it applied to the work world. They know what it feels like to have someone mess with their idea or have it implemented differently from how they envisioned it. In these cases, they know the ripped-off feeling, the exasperation of seeing a great idea being turned into something mediocre. This is exactly what happens at home to many homemakers or stay-at-home parents when someone else's ideas are repeatedly grafted to their own or when plans have to be changed or given up at the last minute. Somehow people working inside the home are supposed to tolerate this interruption of their initiative by loved ones when it would drive anyone else crazy if it happened in the workplace.

Your ideas and hopes for the future are vital for your mental strength. They generate the energy for doing things and give you confidence that you have control in your life. Don't forget that your vitality comes from thinking up ideas, whether simple or profound, and then seeing them through start to finish. Anyone who tries to help by taking over or by making unsolicited suggestions, even a parent or spouse, just doesn't understand that the excitement lies in the autonomy of action, not just in getting the thing done. Have the courage to defend your choices and make plans that follow your instincts. Try rejecting unwanted advice and being a little bullheaded; it's a small price to pay for preventing depression.

Nurture Your Emotional Health

Emotionally immature people admonish you to spend much of your energies on looking after other people. But what about you? Your emotional health depends first upon how you treat yourself. What you think and what you say to yourself are the basis of your psychological well-being. To be happy with your life, first notice how well you look out for yourself.

15 Self-Care Instead of Self-Indulgence

The best self-care often means doing nothing.

Many of us are not great at self-care. While it makes sense to us to feed the dog, put gas in the car, and take care of our family, the concept of taking time for our own maintenance can seem selfish or self-indulgent. The irony is that you are much more likely to act self-indulgently when you *don't* take care of yourself. If you routinely put off emotional and physical self-care, you begin to crave self-indulgences, whether they're good for your health or not. If you keep putting yourself last, no amount of willpower will offset the urge to have as much as you want once you get the chance.

You may be treating your fatigue the way tired parents ignore their screaming toddler in the supermarket. The parent stoically pushes the cart forward, ignoring the child's distress, intent on getting the shopping over with. There's no eye contact, no interaction, just a will to withstand the child's disintegrating emotions and still somehow wind up with groceries in the car.

After a while, that child might give up trying to be heard and instead point to some desirable object and start begging for it. The exhausted parent picks up the item and puts it in the basket, just to bring a moment's peace. Both child and parent somehow seem better after that. The parent has responded to the child. The child feels briefly satisfied. But an indulgence has taken the place of what was really needed: an attentive interaction in which the child feels comforted. Instead, the child's emotional need for parental engagement has been met indirectly through the third-party intercession of, say, Fruit Loops. Tangibles have been substituted for the ineffables of loving connection.

You might act like that parent toward your tired self. Like the harried mother in the supermarket, you may ignore your inner child's signals of distress and focus instead on getting the job done. You push ahead regardless of your fatigue or brain fog. You have to finish before you take a breather because you won't consider resting before the job is complete. You let yourself rest because you're done, not because you're exhausted. You're convinced it will take longer and take *more* work if you give in to your need to stop. So you trick yourself to keep going instead by anticipating that treat you're going to allow yourself later.

Too often, you don't realize that you may be enacting the same inattentive response to your needs that you may have suffered as a child. If your emotional needs were overlooked as a child, your adult fatigue won't matter until you've finished your work. No listening or comfort for you until the job is all done. You push yourself, are impatient with yourself, and make yourself keep going until you're ready to scream inside.

By the time you finally allow yourself to stop, that overwhelmed inner child in you will be emotionally voracious. At that point, you will be desperate for an indulgence. This leads to the binge—the shopping, the impulse purchase, the two or three glasses of wine at the end of the day. It is as if you are saying to yourself, "I can't give you a day off or even an hour of doing what you want—nor can I let you take a break or daydream—*but* I can give you a treat the next chance we get." You feel like you deserve it after ignoring yourself for so long. But why not stop ignoring yourself in the first place?

Human beings need leisure. You need it frequently during the day, not just after five o'clock. As the proverb says, a change is as good as a rest. An effective kind of self-care is to take breaks and do something else for a while. It's no accident that many Silicon Valley companies offer bouncy balls, gyms, ping-pong tables, and bringing your dog to work. People are most energetic in waves of work and play.

The best self-care often means doing nothing. Cozy aimlessness—slipping out of high gear in favor of enjoying downtime—puts you back in touch with your sensory, physical nature. Life takes on an easier rhythm. You feel replenished when you drop out of overdrive and allow your engines to idle. Shifting away from goals and into daydreaming supports creativity and good brain health. When you drop your laser-like focus, your mind moves in more natural patterns, reviewing and integrating your experiences in a relaxed way. Yin and yang, rest and work, self-connection and mission completion—you need both sides. Otherwise, you may crave balance through imbalance: exhaustion followed by indulgence.

Give to yourself along the way. It's not just about scheduling another yoga class. It's about asking yourself sincerely how you're feeling in the moment and reconnecting with your inner state. If you're feeling antsy, it's time to take a break. If you're lonely, maybe it's time to call someone and tell them just that. If you're feeling empty, maybe you need time with your emotional or spiritual self. Giving kindness to what you are feeling will fill you up. Don't keep pushing until the only thing you're looking forward to is that entire box of Fruit Loops. When indulgences look too good, you're probably doing too much. Time to take care of yourself instead.

16   The Importance of Emotional Safety

It's not insecure to want frequent feedback about mattering to our loved ones.

You likely know about the fight, flight, or freeze reactions to fear. But did you know there is also a branch of our nervous system—the ventral vagus nerve—that soothes and restores us to a feeling of safety after we've had a scare? Neuroscientist Stephen Porges explains how this calming part of our nervous system responds to the comforts of social engagement, prompting us to seek safety in others through physical proximity, touch, a soothing voice, or warm facial expressions. These welcoming behaviors from other people don't just tell us we're physically safe; they also tell us we are *emotionally* safe around them.

Emotional safety is not just a feel-good emotion, like whipped cream on a sundae. It arises from the activation of this social engagement nerve, which allows you to connect with others and feel safe. Emotional safety makes you relaxed, open, and willing to express yourself, promoting good humor instead of tension or vigilance. In this state, worry diminishes, and you feel present, grounded, and engaged. You feel most emotionally safe around friendly people or while immersed in an absorbing activity. You may also feel emotionally safe when walking in nature, playing with your dog, or relaxing a few days into your vacation. When your social engagement nerve turns on, you feel a sensation of emotional well-being that brings relaxation and inner contentment.

Lack of emotional safety in childhood can have effects on our adult relationships. It's hard to maintain emotional safety if you are around people whom you find threatening in any way. Growing up with an EI parent creates emotional unsafety even if they weren't physically aggressive due to the stress of their judgment, criticism, or sarcasm signaling the possibility of conflict. Consider how you feel as an adult when you are in an unfriendly situation where the people around you are critical, easily irritated, or have an unwelcoming facial expression. Your nervous system correctly reads such behavior as an unsafe situation and keeps your fight-flight-or-freeze alarm systems ready to go. For a child or an adult, this can result in stress-induced symptoms that compromise your health.

For children, a blank face is not an emotionally neutral experience; it is a potential danger signal. A child's nervous system reads an emotionally unengaged parent as potentially rejecting, a terrifying prospect for a child. Instead of feeling free to reach out to others in a state of trust and calm, such children learn to keep their guard up and be prepared for a quick escape. For these children as adults, anything less than explicit acceptance from others can threaten their sense of emotional safety.

This is why friendly reassurances and engaged attention are so important in your most intimate relationships. It's not insecure to want frequent feedback about mattering to your loved ones; it's a biological urge to move yourself into a safe state of neurological connection. I'm sure you've noticed that people who are the happiest together respond to each other's feelings and requests. Social engagement signals don't have to be flamboyant. The slight crinkling of warm eyes, a passing touch, or a barely discernible nod is all it takes to make you feel seen and safe.

Likewise, you may not realize how much you contribute to other people's neurological well-being when you treat them nicely and give them real smiles. Every time you warmly interact with someone, however briefly, you are literally shifting his or her nervous system into a safe state.

You can strengthen the social engagement branch of your vagal nerve by spending time with pleasant, emotionally responsive people. Warm interactions, however brief, help tone this nerve and contribute to feelings of well-being. Such reassuring contact helps you think better, feel more optimistic, initiate more emotional connections, and enjoy your social activities.

How do you tell who is a safe person for you? You know by how you feel *after* you've been with them. Do you feel happier, lighter, and more hopeful? Or drained, unsatisfied, and stressed? And how do you feel *before* you see them?

Are you looking forward to being with them and feeling happy or dreading it and wishing you could spend your time elsewhere? Your sensations reflect how emotionally safe you feel with that person. Your ventral vagal nerve will tell you who lowers your energy or affects your mood.

If you make a point to fill your life with people who like to engage, you not only will feel emotionally safe, you'll lower your stress too. Time spent in soothing connection is time not spent in fear or stress. Once you've realized how stressful it is not to be emotionally responded to, you will be motivated to find more nourishing relationships. You can always trust your feeling of emotional safety to point you in the right direction.

17 Use Your Health-O-Meter

We clearly need something to make it impossible for us to keep ignoring ourselves.

I wish I were an inventor. If I had an ounce of aptitude in that department, I would be out in my garage at this very moment. With my pliers and soldering iron, I would be making the single most important contribution to mental health ever devised. I would sell them to people at cut-rate prices, flood the internet, and go international.

Imagine a small flat plastic box (new fashion colors every season), thin enough to wear under clothing, lightweight enough to forget about, with skin sensors on the back that people wear like a medication patch. Totally modern, but with an old-fashioned dial-face on the front, one of those half-moon-shaped monitors with a needle that arcs 180 degrees side to side.

Now, somehow—this is the part where I need that electrical engineering degree—this device would test where your emotional focus is at any given moment. The green zone on the left side of the dial would indicate when you are focused on how you feel and what you need. The right side, the red zone, is when you push yourself hard to fix conditions beyond your control, such as other people's emotional states or their life choices.

As you can imagine, parents spend much time in the red zone, worrying about what their kids are going to do next. Someone with a sick loved one might red-zone on a daily basis. In contrast, a person who is absorbed in things they love doing would be hanging out in the green zone. With healthy balance, you would alternate back and forth as needed, but in unhealthy situations, you would spend too much time focused on what other people want.

I would call my invention the Health-o-Meter. This fanciful device would revolutionize mental health because suddenly people would be able to see how much time they spend in a state of self-depriving tension. Like checking one's blood pressure, people could see that they had been keeping themselves in the red zone for, say, two days now, or heaven forbid, for years. This would alert them to do something to get back to the left side of the dial as quickly as possible. Since the Health-o-Meter would be so accurate, they would not be able to fool themselves that cleaning out a closet is as much fun as sitting down with a great book for two hours. Nor would they portray themselves as gladly living to make everybody happy.

· They wouldn't be able to deny their own needs because the Health-o-Meter wouldn't let them. This clever monitor would be fixed up to alert you like a cell phone alarm by emitting a rising crescendo of annoying sound the longer you tried to eke it out in the red zone of self-sacrifice. A little too much niceness, a little too long, would set off an inaudible purr, much like your cell phone's vibrate mode. Keep up the pleasantries beyond your tolerance and the monitor would vibrate with an insistent burring that could be heard by the person beside you. Take responsibility for other people's problems, and the thing would begin to yip like an agitated Chihuahua. Finally, if you put yourself last long enough, the dial-box would emit a rising moan, like an approaching ambulance, until you finally did something for yourself for a change.

Of course, this noisy racket would be highly embarrassing, so you would learn to quietly check your Health-o-Meter at your first twinge of annoyance or emotional fatigue. You would track your emotional energy fluctuations more carefully.

We actually already have a Health-o-Meter now, but it works very slowly and is more easily ignored than my hypothetical invention. Instead of a dial or alarm, our current system creates symptoms over time. It can take years to develop high blood pressure or entrenched depression. In fact, the old way takes so long for the effects to show up that most of the time, we miss the connection. We wonder where our health problems or emotional distress come from, because we are taught that unbalanced self-sacrifice is the mark of a good person living a worthwhile life. Unfortunately, it is more often the mark of a person headed for psychological distress, emotional deadening, and physical breakdown.

To keep ourselves happy and emotionally solvent, we have to avoid red-zoning unnecessarily while seeking as many chances as possible to find pleasure. Our dedication to being honest about what we really feel is the single most energy-giving thing we can do for ourselves.

Many of us tend to go overboard trying to be loving and altruistic. We will work ourselves numb trying to be who others need us to be. We clearly need something to make it impossible for us to keep ignoring ourselves. My fantasy invention may be a long way off, but you can create a Health-o-Meter in your own mind with no effort at all. In every situation, just keep your eye on that imaginary dial and an ear out for your internal alarm. If enough people start doing this, I won't have to go out in my garage at all.

18   Writing Therapy

Be illogical, desperate, but truthful.

Worst case scenario: You are facing an awful dilemma. You are scared, confused, desperate. Nobody understands you. You don't understand you. There are no therapists available. Quick, what do you do?

If you had an emergency handbook for such moments, you could look it up fast under "Going Nuts." Right there, under the heading "Equipment Required," it would say, "Your own brain," and under the section "First Step," it would say, "Get pen and paper." Putting the contents of your mind down on paper should be in every home's first aid manual as the best response to overwhelming situations. It is the single most effective self-help method you can use when circumstances have outrun your ability to keep up.

Modern life is very action-driven and promotes swift responses to challenges as the ideal way of stopping problems and regaining control. Unfortunately, there are plenty of situations in human living—especially involving other people—in which a quick response actually makes things worse.

When you are getting nowhere with your actions, it may be because you don't know what is *really* upsetting you. When you take action before you know your true feelings, your blind reactions create mayhem around you. Now you have a second problem to deal with caused by reacting impulsively to the first problem!

Instead of jumping into action, sit down with some notebook paper and write freely. Write sloppy and fast, eschewing punctuation, grammar, and capitalization. Plan to shred it when you are through. Nobody is reading it but you. Be illogical, desperate, but truthful. What is your worst fear about the situation? What do you secretly wish you could do? What does this horrible, terrible situation remind you of? How are you feeling about yourself? Why? What are you seeing that you have not let yourself admit? Once you know the deeper essentials, you are in a much better position to deal with the problem.

Why does this work? Because writing—even sloppy, distraught writing—requires your brain activity to move out of primitive emotional centers and route itself up through the higher, frontal parts of the brain where language, meaning, and insight live. As far as the brain is concerned, your writing is an evolutionary stage above your feeling.

In research studies, writing has been shown to decrease depression but only if people used the writing to address their problems. Writing about neutral, impersonal topics had no effect. It is not just the writing act itself that is therapeutic; it is trying to get at the emotional truth that seems to work.

Small children always need to express their hurt feelings and fears before they can be truly comforted. Blurting it out is the first step toward solving any emotional dilemma. If we can do that, even on paper, it speeds up solution-finding—much better than digging through an avalanche of impulsive reactions afterward.

Unless there is immediate danger, consider exploring your own brain before you explore the outside options available to you. A bout of frenzied writing will often hit the heart of the matter, making you stop and sit back, stunned by the nakedness of an unmet need or childhood fear. Once you have found the core of your emotional reaction, think about it, kiss it right on top of its head, then sit back and figure out what to do about it. With more of your brain involved, you are bound to do a better job.

19 Learning from Nature

Nature is enthusiastic about individuality.

Every time I face a major dilemma in life, I seek out nature. It is an ancient urge to return to something wiser than myself. If I can walk in nature or just go outside, the noise falls away and leaves clarity behind. It's as if my brain needs to commune with nature's peaceful, evolving order to come up with the best way forward. In nature, it seems right to focus just on me and what I truly need.

Unlike an EI parent, nature is enthusiastic about individuality. Nothing is uniform. Everything has its own unique expression. Nature's rampant individuality reflects and intensifies the experience of your own true being. You feel more alive in nature because you sense your value in the grand scheme of things. You find yourself taking on a wider perspective that calms and strengthens. For instance, standing in a grove of trees is like finding yourself among a remarkable group of beings who are totally and fully at ease with themselves and have no need for you to be anything other than what you are too.

When you observe nature and find her beautiful, you enter into a circle of appreciation between living things. This is not so strange if you consider that all life probably started from a common source and developed into different forms through adaptations over eons. I think life still recognizes itself, whether it ended up as a plant or as a human being. When you walk in nature, you are among friends whose ancestors are intertwined with yours. You are fellow flourishers from the oldest days of this planet.

Let's not forget that you are organic too. You are as carbon-based as the trees, and, like them, we humans evolved as life-forms growing and adapting in the air and sunshine. The way nature looks now is a living record of that adaptive process. Just like a tree or a blade of grass, you will also gravitate toward the nutrients available around you. You start to wilt when you're in the wrong place, but once you make the right adjustments, you will perk back up again. No wonder wise decisions and choices arise more naturally as you let nature speak to your core.

Unfortunately, you can lose touch with what you need and what you should stay away from. Instead, you may have migrated up into your head—perhaps the last significant migration of the human species—to emphasize thinking instead of knowing your heart. When you have problems, you now believe you should sit down and figure them out like a student at your desk. You think that everything must be learned through your rational, logical brain and that nothing worthwhile is produced from just enjoying calmness on a daily basis. But in fact, this steady peacefulness is how all of natural life was formed: a graceful, accommodating response to every environmental challenge.

When you force yourself to think hard at problem-solving, you use a part of your brain that tires quickly, especially when you are anxious. Pushing hard for a solution may give you lists of pros and cons, but these don't necessarily get you to the crux of the issue. By overusing this intense part of your brain, you end up tired, frustrated, and often in a bad mood. The strain of worry and problem-solving depletes your feel-good chemicals.

Your logical, rational mind likes straight lines, right angles, and efficiencies. It pushes you toward fast decisions to make sure you don't waste time or resources. It's a crimped approach that believes the best decision-making is the shortest line between two points. But straight lines are rare in nature, more likely to be found in minerals than in living things. Forcing your mind exclusively into these unnatural forms disrupts the flow of your natural creativity and resourcefulness.

In fact, effort and efficiency never guarantee good decisions. Nature shows you a different but wildly successful approach. Nature is friendly with time and isn't pushed by it. Living more naturally takes your energy stores into account by seeking the most rewarding route, not the most direct route. Nature isn't impressed by straight lines. Its style is easy and opportunistic.

Nature is the source of your subconscious mind, the place where your creativity, inspiration, and dreams come from. This part of your mind is like a growing vine, sending out shoots and leaves in an unhurried, elegant fashion as it heads for the sunlight and food. It reaches for the top in accordance with what it has soaked up from the bottom. It doesn't push itself to grow past the limits of its nurturance as we humans are often expected to do. Nature lives by the rule that output is balanced by input. When you forget this, you exhaust yourself, resulting in anxiety and poor health. Nature shows you that everything you see aboveground depends on what was nurtured underground.

Do you follow that rule—that for every advance there must be a replenishment of energies and rest? Or do you treat yourself like a machine, continually forcing yourself ahead?

Being in nature reconnects you with your origins and needs. Nature is so true to itself that it rubs off on you. It encourages your healthy instincts and guides you forward with the least resistance. It shows you that you can have a vibrant life just by being yourself. It's like a kindly, wise parent who wants only your best. It is, after all, your Mother Nature.

PART II

Dealing with People

Relationship Issues

If it seems that relationships hold the key to your happiness, you may not realize that your primary relationship has to be to yourself. Once you've accomplished that, you're ready for other people. Whether it's a friendship or romance, look for someone who respects your boundaries, honors your individuality, and tries to understand you. Respecting each other's uniqueness opens doors to even deeper connections.

20 The Relationship Economy

It's a mistake to think you should be adult enough to settle for less than you want.

People often assume that good relationships take hard work. It is amazing to me what a grim and joyless impression many people have of committed relationships. They make it sound like the goal of a relationship should be to try your patience, not increase your happiness. But the point of having a relationship is what it can add to your life, not what it takes away. Thoughtful, clear communication shouldn't feel like hard work. If it feels like effort to get along with your partner, maybe that's not normal.

Committed relationships in our culture are often characterized as being high in responsibility and low in personal autonomy. The cliché is promoted that loss of freedom and less happiness is the inescapable price of being a grown-up in a long-term relationship. As a result, many people enter commitments willing to put up with way too much and get way too little in return. It's a mistake to think you should be adult enough to settle for less than you want. No wonder so many long-term commitments ultimately collapse. It's an unsustainable economy.

Sooner or later, when people are working hard in their relationships and still not getting what they want, they may opt to leave. And they will leave with bitterness because they will feel betrayed by the cultural promise that self-sacrifice and infinite patience should have brought them happiness. But relationships are just like any other exchange. What you put into them is not necessarily what you get out of them. No matter how hard you work or what you give up, you can't force another person to reciprocate. Psychological maturity and generosity are what determine a person's level of reciprocity—not how much you give. Consider proof in your own experience, such as giving endlessly to an EI parent and receiving little back.

In good relationships, it's true that not every trade is fair nor every compromise equally satisfying. Over time, however, it should even out so that each person's investment is yielding a return. In the bartering of an intimate relationship, if I give you a sheep and you offer me an apple, I'm going to notice the inequity. If I am okay with the apple this time, it probably means I know you're good for a sheep down the road. There's a sense of fairness being observed by both parties, without unrealistic attitudes of entitlement.

Increased energy should also be a benefit of a good relationship. To feel energized by a person's company means that contact with them usually leaves you feeling lighter, brighter, and in better spirits. Your relationship partner should enrich you, not tire you. People who energize others keep up their own energy by doing things they enjoy. They look for opportunities to have fun and thereby strengthen their interest and vitality. When partners are taking care of themselves, they each bring good energy to the relationship. The synergy builds, and interactions feel rewarding to both.

But if emotional hard work and too many unfair trades characterize the relationship, like it may have with your EI parent, your energy will sink. The trade balance is too uneven.

Another erroneous ideal is that you shouldn't keep score in a committed relationship. Somehow true love is supposed to be above that. But can you imagine a real human being not keeping score at some level? It is much better to keep track of relative effort so things can be equaled out if partners feel they are giving more than they are receiving. If you point out unfairness to a person who wants to be fair, no offense is taken. Instead, that person will be interested and concerned. It is only a person with an overblown sense of entitlement who takes offense when unfair treatment is pointed out.

In addition to fairness and reciprocity, a good partner is easy to talk to and makes you feel understood. This isn't about complicated conversing; it's just a simple willingness to listen like you count too. Does the person get it when you explain that the relationship trade agreement is feeling bad on your end?

The feeling that you can talk frankly about problems is one of the best ways to predict how rewarding the relationship will be. Your partner's attitude toward communication predicts how hard your relationship work will be. If the person reacts angrily or withdraws and avoids, then it certainly will be hard work—just to feel stable.

You will feel more optimistic and competent in any kind of committed relationship if you see its underlying structure as a trade economy. That's not unromantic, just realistic. If you want to keep your relationship healthy in the long run, keep in mind the rules of all trade: give as much as you want, but ask for enough in return that it feels fair to you both.

21 The Gumby Effect

Character is not who you are when you try hard; it is who you are when there's nothing to gain.

People are psychologically stretchy. I call this the Gumby effect after the green rubber toy that can be pulled all kinds of ways, always to return to its original shape. When we try hard, we are all able to stretch beyond what's comfortable and briefly look better than we really are. The Gumby effect allows us to be overachievers for short bursts of time. But when the pressure is off, we return to form.

In relationships, when people are trying their best to make a good first impression, they enlarge themselves like Gumby in stretch mode. But then Gumby shrinks back to normal size as the person relaxes the stretch and sinks back into who he or she is at their core. Think of Gumby in his normal shape as a person's real level of psychological maturity. Once matured, we hold our shape in a way we don't have to think about. Like Gumby, once people reach their maximum development, their personalities don't change much. However, when people don't fully develop psychologically, they have to compensate for their emotional immaturity by learning to stretch in order to look good and get what they want.

Many people get to know their partner when that person is trying hard to make a good impression. In Gumby terms, the partner is stretching mightily. In the early days, the partner might have done thoughtful things, professed love, or showed tender sympathy. But over time, the stretch wears thin and then contracts to a more comfortable shape. That's when you see their true form.

If you meet someone in stretch mode, you will think they are more emotionally available than they really are. When they recoil back to their true shape, you may wonder where that wonderful person went. They suddenly seem more selfish, less sensitive, more defensive, more fault-finding, and more controlling. In short, they begin to show their immature shape, their true Gumby form.

When Gumby people shrink back into their comfort zone, you might think they *could* return to their previous marvelous self if only they really tried. That's true enough. But who lives daily life trying hard? It's a mistake to think of the selfish behavior as a choice or that the person could be nicer if he or she wanted to. Such people don't stay mature because they can't, just like a child on good behavior can't keep it up forever. You can't get past the physics of a stretch; it's only a temporary state.

When you meet emotionally immature people in stretch mode, you won't be able to see right away that they are incapable of sustaining their good appearance. Only time and experience with them will tell you that. The best approach is to give the relationship time to develop so that you can see whether their caring behavior is Gumby overachievement or their real functioning. Metaphorically, is that person really that tall, or are they stretching on tiptoe?

This is particularly true in the area of emotional intimacy, where people open up and communicate with each other about their deepest needs, feelings, and dreams. In the early days of a relationship, Gumby people will stretch themselves into a more expanded version of themselves, putting effort into listening and caring. But there will always be moments when Gumby snaps back into the original shape, if only for a second. That snap-back moment is a preview of whom you will be living with.

Ask yourself if your new love interest is kind and reliable in a relaxed way over the long haul or just when stretching for the moment. Are you seeing true kindness and caring in them, or is it the temporary exertion of a more immature personality, sure to retract under the next period of sustained stress?

The answer to this question is not immediate because Gumby's expansion fatigue takes time to show up. It is the best reason for not jumping into commitments too fast. Gumby types always pressure you for quick decisions and commitments because it's a strain to be nice for so long. They try to bag you quickly so they can contract back into a more comfortable shape.

In old-fashioned terms, the opposite of the Gumby effect is *character*. It refers to who you are when there is nothing to be gained from acting otherwise. Character is not who you are when you try hard; it is who you are when there's nothing to gain. Like Gumby, you can't tell a person's real shape when ulterior motives are pulling them this way and that. Let them relax and feel like they've got you, and then see how they behave.

We can never afford to stop asking ourselves this question about new people in our lives: Is this who this person really is, or are they stretching hard? It can be a long and painful process to extricate yourself from a frustrating relationship once you have fallen for the Gumby effect because you keep hoping that the next stretch will stick. But step back and observe the shape they resume when nothing's at stake. Watch how they treat you when they're confident they have you. That's the real Gumby.

22 The Café of Love

If we already need someone we don't really know, the potential for letdown is huge.

Finding a mate can be like trying a new restaurant. In the Café of Love, do we read the menu prior to committing in order to avoid painful disillusionment later on? Or do we walk in the door and tell the server to bring us whatever he likes? Sometimes, if we're really hungry, some of us dispense with the menu altogether. In the Café of Love, we not only let our waiter decide—we pay in advance, fat tip included, then eagerly hope we'll get something we like.

We can afford to be selective only when we are already emotionally well fed. When we're famished after a childhood with an EI parent, any restaurant is a welcome sight. We're not too picky as long as it has a nice facade and parking near the door. We barely take time to check the menu.

But the real problem is not what's on the menu. The deeper problem occurs when we're too impatient to read the menu. We sit down at the table already starving. We latch onto the other person immediately, *needing* them before we even *know* them. If we already need someone we don't really know, the potential for letdown is huge.

While the answer to the problem seems obvious—take time to read the menu and get to know the person—it doesn't seem to work that way. We like to fall in love first and ask questions later. We even rationalize inconsiderate behavior and don't see what's obvious to others. Of course, by then, we are probably in deep and thinking this is the only place left on earth to eat. Then we are in for a long, painful process of leaving someone to whom we gave our heart before we knew this person could be trusted with it.

Usually the signs of trouble were there from the beginning. We were just too hungry to look for them. As with packaged food, the ingredients of potential partners are listed in their micro-behaviors—how they treat you when they think you're not looking. In grocery stores, a product's ingredients will tell you whether it's nourishing or just packaged to look good. It's the same with seductive people. Looking attractive doesn't mean they're good for you. You might end up with a candy bar instead of a meal.

Bad partners, like nonnutritive foods, only seem irresistible when we are emotionally starved. We let ourselves get too hungry by going unnurtured too long. Then, like an emaciated castaway, everything starts to look like food. Eye contact, flirting, or other signs of interest are quickly misinterpreted as hors d'oeuvres promising a full-fledged banquet. We don't stop to ask ourselves whether a banquet is actually available, and we certainly aren't rude enough to ask if these hors d'oeuvres might be all we ever get. Right around the time when we hope to be digging into our relational entrée, the potential partner pulls back or starts causing fights. Is there any way to see this coming?

Yes, but only if we *want* to see it coming. Our emotional hunger makes us hope for safety and commitment long before anything is really there. We are afraid to check the menu for fear no entrées are listed—which would feel disastrous because we've decided this is the person who will finally fill us up.

Many potential partners make for good hors d'oeuvres. Their initial attentiveness takes the edge off our hunger enough so that we can start getting choosy about the rest of the meal. After we've had a snack, we start to notice spots on the silverware or the fact that the waiter keeps bringing us undercooked food. But as long as you're terribly hungry, you'll make excuses for the inexcusable.

Starvation does not make you a food critic; it just makes you enthusiastic about substandard fare. Before you can be discerning about potential partners, you have to care enough about yourself not to put up with being let down. Once you care enough to feed yourself with friendships, interests, and activities, junk food won't look so great. You'll hold out for high-quality nourishment with a nice presentation.

When you feel satisfied with yourself, only kind, equally engaged people with a good sense of humor will spark your appetite. You'll look past the powdered sugar on top and ask, *Did their behavior consider my feelings?* You'll curb romantic fantasies until you see if there's anything underneath. You'll notice if they are nutritionally dense or self-serving and dry.

As with good food, selecting quality relationships requires an experienced palate. If you make the connection between the first taste and how your tummy feels later on, empty calories will lose their pull. In the Café of Love, you'll start choosing nourishing people who offer emotional nutrition, satiety, and feelings of strength and energy. Like food, some people are sustaining, and some people are strictly for fun. Your job is to read their labels, discover which is which, and make sure you're not too hungry before you go out.

23 Mr. and Ms. Right Now

When a rigid life role has gotten too frustrating, the inner self starts agitating for something new.

Recently, a friend was telling a group of us about the time her car broke down on the side of the interstate. The guy who pulled up behind her to help was clearly my friend's opposite in culture, politics, and general orientation to life. But my friend was never so glad to see someone in her life. The guy changed the flat, refused an offer of money for his services, and went on his way. Another person in our group laughed and said, "Well, he may not have been Mr. Right, but he sure was Mr. Right Now!"

I love this story because it is so true that people we might not associate with at one point in our lives suddenly can appear at the right moment to bring us just what we need. My friend previously would not have chosen to hang out with her highway benefactor, but that had nothing to do with the profound gratitude she felt in receiving his help. The bonds we form in breakdowns bypass stereotypes and go straight to the heart.

People who are very different from us often come into our lives to show us what we need in order to develop. There is no place where this is more true than in romantic relationships. You might form an intense attraction to someone who enters your life during times of personal change and inner transition. Because your old way of being has broken down, it hardly matters who stops to help you. During such times, even long-term relationships can be rocked by outside infatuations.

When relationship upheavals happen, you wonder what in the world is going on. Why do previously responsible people blow up their orderly lives? Why are you suddenly ready to give up everything for a new guy or gal who may look to others like nothing more than Mr. or Ms. Wrong?

Blame it on your psyche's infallible instinct for balance. When a rigid life role has gotten too frustrating, the inner self starts agitating for something new. It wants you to satisfy your whole self, not just the social script you might have followed up to that point. This inner demand for growth wants you to stop pretending to be content and discover your true self by trying something new. Sometimes this innocent desire to grow attracts you to a person who is the walking incarnation of some disavowed part of yourself.

Your growth instinct is not exactly telling you to have an affair or date the guy with the Mohawk or the gal in the skintight jeans, but sometimes the message gets garbled as it comes through. Instead of recognizing that you need to express a new side of *yourself,* you may think you have found the answer in that quirky new person who treats you like you're the greatest.

We could call all these guys and gals Mr. or Ms. Right Now. They may not be Mr. or Ms. Right for the long haul, but they were interested enough to stop and ask how you are. In these unlikely relationships, you finally feel you can own who you are inside and what you want from life. You open up to possibilities that previous conformities forbade you. If someone's attentions boost your vital connection to your emotional and instinctual self, it can be hard to resist. Other people may be baffled by the attraction, but often it reflects how desperate you are to find some way back to your neglected soul. You are not looking for Mr. or Ms. Right but for yourself.

If Mr. or Ms. Right Now shows up when everyone else is taking you for granted, is it any surprise when you leap at the chance? Whether you are a teenager, an adult, or a midlife cruiser, the fleeting pleasures of right now can feel like a fair trade for years of conformity.

Unfortunately, the Mr. and Ms. Right Nows of the world make you forget that happiness is an inside job and that fulfillment comes from self-actualization, not just getting a new boyfriend or girlfriend. When swept off your feet, you need to remember that sooner or later, those are the same two feet you will have to stand up on all by yourself. Mr. or Ms. Right Now may seem to promise to do all your self-discovery for you. But what do you really get out of that? They may inspire you to change your life, but their job can never be to tell you which way you need to go.

It helps to think about what was going on in your life when Mr. or Ms. Right Now started looking so good. Chances are that the new person has many of the qualities you have repressed in yourself. Instead of mistaking roadside assistance for a soul mate, it might be a good idea to wonder if Mr. or Ms. Right Now represents what you need to express in yourself.

24 Should I Stay, or Should I Go?

You may sense that you are not just leaving the relationship, but leaving your own dependency.

We can be quick to tell others to drop unhappy relationships without understanding why the person is in such a relationship in the first place. Thinking about leaving a relationship of any type is a process of awakening, no matter what the circumstances. Anyone thinking about leaving a marriage, job, or friendship is beginning to question the belief that they exist for the needs of others. Leaving an unhappy relationship, therefore, is not the straightforward question of whether you should stay or go; it is the deep psychological choice of whether or not you feel entitled to live a happy life.

When you are ambivalent about leaving a bad situation, you might be financially dependent or have children to consider, but as the child of an EI parent you may be overly focused on the feelings and needs of others. You can be terribly distressed yet overlook this as you worry about the hurt or anger you may cause other people. It can take a long time to make this shift from prioritizing the feelings of others to waking up to the reality of your own unhappiness.

When you say, "Should I stay or go?" you are really asking whether or not it is okay to take power back over your own life. You may not feel you can be a self-assured, forthright person *and* stay in the relationship. You are so used to considering others that you might believe you have to leave a relationship in order to be yourself.

Indecision is often a deeper ambivalence about claiming personal power, and that is what makes it so hard to leave. You may sense that you are not just leaving the relationship but leaving your own dependency. This dependency can take many forms, but basically it is the dependency upon the approval of others and the feeling that your existence is only valuable if you are needed by others.

Whenever you're thinking of leaving a relationship—whether a marriage, friendship, or job—you will do so more peacefully if you give yourself adequate time to come to grips with all the meanings such a move will have. It is no failure to be indecisive, or even to leave and come back and then leave and come back again. All this back and forth is your psyche's way of dealing with enormous doubts about the right to be an individual and claim personal power over your life. Sometimes a huge amount of ambivalence is unavoidable until it becomes clear what you want and why.

Just remember that as you struggle in your indecision, you are growing inside, even though no one can see it, even you. Every time you make the mental circuit of the reasons why you want your freedom, you get a little stronger, a little more accustomed to the idea. When you are finally ready on the inside, the steps in the outside world come easier. In fact, when you are truly ready to go, leaving has a calmness and a fullness to it that is distinctive. Because you take the time you need to feel confident about your move, you often have fewer regrets or second thoughts later.

When you can't decide whether to stay or go, give yourself the time and self-acceptance necessary to come to a decision that feels solid. You should never feel rushed by other people or someone else's idea of what it means to be strong. Real strength and resolution come from working through an issue, not just taking action. Staying or going is not the most basic decision; it is really about deciding to be yourself or not.

25 Be a Relationship Leader

If you wait for people to guess your needs, relationships fall apart.

Good relationships require taking the lead sometimes. Most of us have had a few less-than-stellar relationships, but we tend to accept things as they are rather than guiding the relationship to a healthier place. We assume we are stuck with how the other person is. More likely, we haven't thought through what we really want from the relationship. We default to reacting passively in our relationships instead of taking leadership.

EI parents teach their children to follow them without question, so you may have been trained to be overly passive at times in your relationships. But if you wait for people to guess your needs, relationships fall apart. Instead of being annoyed by other people's insensitivity, it works better to tell them what you want them to do. What kind of responses would you like from them?

Such open communication comes more naturally in close friendships and intimate relationships. But you can also lead in other relationships that you didn't choose, such as your work, neighbors, and family connections. Even when you end up around people with whom you have little in common—and who don't notice how you feel or what you want—you can shine as a relationship leader.

Relationship leaders are people who are clear about how they want to be treated and what makes their relationships rewarding. They request respectful treatment, such as asking people to be polite or to disagree without being insulting. For instance, a relationship leader might say to someone who barks orders, "I'd love to help you, and I'd love for you to ask me nicely." Or to a person who mocks others' political views, a relationship leader might say, "I think it's perfectly fine when people see things differently, and it's interesting to hear both sides." These are neutral responses that actively lift the dialogue toward something better.

Relationship leaders can even go a step further by offering ideas for how relationships can be made more rewarding for *both* parties. For example, people who annoy you by coming by whenever they feel like it may seem disrespectful of boundaries. You might make a request, such as "Please call before you come to see if I'm up for a visit." But you could also offer relational leadership by sharing a general truth about good relationships, like "Getting a heads-up is nice in case someone's in the middle of something" or "Visits are more fun when both people are ready to socialize."

If people violate a boundary you requested, they are telling you they didn't take it seriously the first time. They are still stuck on their own wishes, so they need your leadership toward more desirable behavior. For instance, if a coworker keeps talking after you've stated your need for uninterrupted work time, you can lead the relationship by saying, "To be good coworkers, we have to give each other time to get things done. Let me get back to you when I'm able to talk." To an angry friend, you could say, "I'm sorry you're upset, and I hope we can resolve this. It's good that you can be honest with me." In a respectful, informative way, you are offering good relationship values to live by.

Beyond setting limits, there may be times when other people simply treat you badly or accuse you of things that aren't true. That's when relationship leadership can guide the relationship forward without reacting in ways that could injure the bond beyond repair. For example, if someone unjustly accuses you of a malevolent intent, you might say, "That's not how I meant it," and follow up with relational leadership, such as "Let's check in with each other before assuming the worst" or, if someone has been holding a grudge against you, "Things work better if we clearly tell each other why we're upset."

Sometimes adult children and their parents, whether emotionally immature or not, have conflicts over competing interests. Since parents are accustomed to being the authority figures, it often falls to the adult child to lead the way to a more equal and respectful adult relationship. For instance, when parents try to take over or give advice, you might say, "Well, that's a good idea, Mom, but it's important for me to think this through for myself." If a parent gets angry and speaks harshly, you can be the leader by saying, "I expect you to control yourself. We are two grown adults now. How are we going to have a good adult relationship with you talking to me like that?"

Remember, the ultimate goal of relationship leadership is not only to speak up for yourself but also to offer reminders of relationship values that can inspire both of you to treat each other respectfully. Your choice is either to lead or follow. It's not doing them any favors if you know a better way but don't teach them a better way.

26 Why Emotional Maturity Matters

The other person's emotional maturity is crucial in considering any new venture.

Sometimes we have to grant others power over us such as when we apply for a new job, select a new teacher or leader, or enter into a legal partnership. The level of emotional maturity in these important figures can make a huge difference in your quality of life.

For instance, emotional maturity in leaders means that they can care about something or someone outside of themselves. It also means they can deal with reality on its own terms, show empathy for others, and demonstrate self-reflection and accountability. Such a leader or boss can be trusted to take responsibility, fix their mistakes, and take into account how others think and feel.

People in positions of power, such as parents, bosses, teachers, and leaders need emotional maturity because so much of their job requires being fair and caring for others. EI people have trouble with both of these things. Being fair and caring for others run against the grain of an immature person's prime directive to meet his or her own needs first. To be under the control of an emotionally immature person is miserable; that's why the other person's emotional maturity is crucial in considering any new venture.

People in power are capable of fairness when they can step outside themselves and imagine not only what is best for them but what will be good for others too. Emotionally mature people do this naturally. They feel uneasy when something is unfair to someone, even if the imbalance might be to their benefit. They have a basic sense that other people—at some fundamental, human level—deserve fair treatment too.

EI people, on the other hand, are so self-preoccupied that they instinctively take advantage of others. They're often oblivious to what others go through because they're unable to emotionally imagine other people's experiences. They lack the multidimensionality in their personality to wonder what it's like for the person who is being treated unfairly. As long as it's not happening to them, they have no urge to stand in someone else's shoes. They may try to act concerned, but inevitably, EI bosses, leaders, or business associates will do something so surprisingly egocentric that you realize how little they consider the welfare of other people. This trait usually comes out when a big issue is at stake, but you can be sure there were countless little signs earlier when they showed their lack of true caring.

When we have that foundational sense of being cared for, it creates an atmosphere of security and empowerment. To be your best, you need to feel that people who have power over you can handle reality, treat you fairly, and feel for what you're going through. These abilities originate solely from their level of emotional maturity. For the emotionally mature boss or leader, we are all in this together. For the emotionally immature, we are all in it for them.

When you are considering a commitment to people who will have a measure of control over your life, look at the following: Are they realistic enough? Do they show fairness, especially in the little things? Do you feel cared about in a basic human sense? Do they listen to your point of view as well? If you are working with people like this, you will get the best out of yourself because you will feel safe and secure. Fairness, being valued, and empathic attunement bring out our best talents and energies. Emotional maturity brings contentment, not only to the people who have it, but also to the people who must live around them. When you partner with people who can care about you, everyone is lifted up together. You are more than a means to someone else's success. When it's necessary to grant power to others, make sure you give it to those who want to protect your well-being along with their own.

Difficult People

Difficult people can be blind to your inner experiences. Interactions with them are often frustrating, exhausting, and even depressing. Don't let any passivity you learned as a child give them permission to rule you. You can lessen their control and take action on your own behalf once you understand how to handle them.

27 Dominating Types

They don't want an improved relationship; they want to win.

On the *Dog Whisperer* television show, Cesar Millan invariably has to educate dog owners about dominance in the canine world. Much of Millan's work involves training owners to become the dominant pack leader when their dog attempts to take over. Most of the owners show a surprised "I had no idea" look on their faces when Millan explains how their weak demeanor tempts their dog to seize power.

I must admit, the first few times I watched the show, I too saw the dog's misbehavior as frightened or pathological. It did not occur to me that the dog was being *dominant,* especially when it was a small dog. I probably missed it because, like the pet owners, I tend to think of dogs as furry children in need of nurturing and affection. Why are we so blind to dominance as the central issue?

Perhaps we do not recognize dominance behavior in our pets because we have been trained not to notice it in humans. Frans de Waal, in his book *Our Inner Ape,* notes that the subject of dominance is chronically omitted in human behavioral research. In the psychological field, we might call dominant behavior *narcissism* or *psychopathy* or *intermittent rage disorder.* But we're reluctant to call it by its proper name from the animal world. We humans fool ourselves that normality is being cooperative with others, when nothing is more common than a power grab. It is easier for an animal expert to see dominant behavior for what it is: one entity exerting control over another in order to achieve alpha-leader status.

In human families, dominant members often rule the roost not with nips or bites, but psychologically. Your EI parent may have lorded over you like this, often keeping their position through intimidation, subtle or otherwise, or by inducing feelings of guilt, shame, and inferiority. These dominant alphas bulldoze over anybody who values harmony above status—all for his or her own good, of course.

People with dominant personalities usually do not see their behavior as aggressive. They see themselves as smart and protective, full of advice and knowing what's what. If you were to label them dominating, they would feel deeply misunderstood because they think they are just doing what's best. They seriously believe that any group would benefit from having *them* at the top of the hierarchy.

Actually, they're right about the need for a leader. In any successful pack of animals, leadership is a necessity. Calmness and security are only possible when we know who's running things. Without someone willing to take charge, break up fights, and tell everyone where they stand, animals and humans both would be in a state of existential insecurity all the time. But leadership is not only about dominance; it is about caring for each individual's good as well. If a dog or a person is an unfair or aggressive leader, the whole group suffers. A bad leader dog might end up losing his alpha rank. An overbearing alpha human might find himself or herself fired or in a divorce.

Dominant people have many similarities to animal alphas. People, like apes and dogs, cling to dominance once they have attained it and will fight hard to keep it, even if they would actually be happier without the pressure. Dominant people tend to be suspicious and hypercritical because they feel safe only when finding weaknesses in potential rivals—and everyone, even their children, is a potential rival. They are fanatics about denying their own weaknesses so that upstarts will not take advantage. This is why discussions about their behavior do not work with them. They don't want an improved relationship; they want to win.

In male primates, dominance means intimidating behavior. In primate females, dominance might be more subtle, accomplished through deliberately withholding acceptance and comfort. They might refuse to share or snub some members of the group. In the human world, females have the additional options of guilt-induction and criticisms.

When you live with dominant personalities, you end up doing a lot of emotional work, especially if you were raised by a dominating EI parent. As a result, you are apt to feel very fatigued from catering to the iron-willed alphas in your life. It is tiring to always be thinking about how the alpha person will react. But energy and hope can be rekindled when you realize you don't have to act weak simply because someone enjoys being top dog.

Once dominance is seen for what it is—an insistent drive to be in control—it's possible not to take dominant behavior personally. For instance, if someone is critical or snubs you, it might work better to call it what it is, a dominance move, rather than questioning your own self-worth.

Dominant behavior has only one goal: to diminish you so that alphas can keep their power and rank. It is as basic, and freeing, as that. The dog whisperer knows a power move when he sees one. You can too.

28 Tyrannical Talkers

Their conversation is like being forced to listen to someone reading the local news from an out-of-town newspaper.

Maybe it's just an introvert issue, but I wonder how many of you suffer from people who won't stop talking. I don't mean the garrulous, friendly types who take the lead in a conversation and keep things going. I mean the kind of person whose conversation feels like a runaway truck on the downside of a mountain road. Nothing can stop it.

I call them "tyrannical talkers" because of the driven, controlling quality to their speech. The words keep coming as they react to their own thoughts. They obsess out loud about irrelevant details, such as trying to remember someone's last name, how that person was related to someone else, or the exact date when something happened. Yet you, the listener, couldn't possibly be interested in straightening out these people's memories, nor does it matter to you who's who or precisely when something occurred. Their conversation is like being forced to listen to someone reading the local news from an out-of-town newspaper—one fact after another about people you've never heard of.

These talkers prevent other people from getting a word in edgewise. They do this as artfully as a trained singer, managing their inhalations so that it never feels like there is an opening for you to interject a comment or change of subject. As they catch their breath, they hold the floor with a lingering "and…" or "um…" or "so…," making you forcefully interrupt them if you are going to say anything at all. These place-holding words fool you into thinking that something important is about to be said. With the tyrannical talker, that is almost never true.

The speech of the tyrannical talker is compulsive, driven from within with no input from other people. There is no awareness that they're boring others, talking too long, or not sharing the conversational time. In fact, they proceed as if there were all the time in the world, like nobody is going anywhere or has anything else to do.

Their apparent goal is to hold your attention for as long as possible. In this way, you can see the emotional immaturity of their need. It is not the adult enjoyment of reciprocal conversation; it is more like the anxiety of an emotionally neglected child who dares not stop talking or Mommy won't pay any attention at all. Not trusting that other people will be interested in what they have to say, they sew up the interaction from the outset, keeping the attention on themselves no matter what. It is a self-absorbed social style that holds a captive audience—but only in the short run. Other people quickly learn to manage the dosage with these people, avoiding them or making sure an escape route is available. Tyrannical talkers don't realize they are losing the chance for real, emotionally satisfying interactions. They seem to fear they will become invisible if they stop talking.

If you think you might have some tyrannical talker tendencies, ask yourself if you give other people a chance to speak by leaving pauses and asking questions. A good rule of thumb is that if you have spoken the equivalent of a paragraph, make a little concluding remark to cue others to speak. Be sure to ask at least two questions per conversation about the other person and then listen for at least thirty seconds.

However, if you are usually on the receiving end of tyrannical talkers, ask yourself if you are aiding and abetting their socially exhausting behavior. As a child of an EI parent, were you taught to let others take over conversation because your parent was impatient with what you had to say? Have you been too willing to be too polite, even when your own needs are screaming inside?

If so, you can use the tyrannical talker to help you correct your tendency toward self-effacement. Tyrannical talkers are great people on whom to practice assertive self-expression. Tyrannical talkers are so self-preoccupied they will hardly notice nor take offense if you break into their monologue with thoughts of your own. They are Teflon when it comes to social correction. You can practice speaking up over and over, and they will keep plowing ahead, giving you an excellent workout of your God-given right to speak up on your own behalf.

Remember, you have the right to be heard, not just seen, and tyrannical talkers can be just the ticket for your recovery. Speak up. Raise your voice to interject or redirect the conversation to something interesting to you. Tyrannical talkers, just like the anxious child, might secretly thank you for taking the control out of their hands.

29 The Cold Shoulder

By responding actively, you can refuse the guilt.

Of all the things people can do to each other, the cold shoulder is right up there with the worst. We usually think about punishment as physical pain or deprivation. But in any kind of relationship, giving someone the cold shoulder causes unique hurt. When we ignore others and reject their overtures, we make them feel ashamed and powerless.

The cold shoulder is usually pointed and blatant. You feel frozen out, and it's very clear that the person is angry and disapproves of you. The most insidious effect of the cold shoulder is that often you don't know what you did wrong, leaving you to obsess over your possible misdeeds.

Other forms of the cold shoulder are subtler and make you wonder if you're crazy for thinking something's wrong. You sense a coolness even though the person appears pleasant and even chipper, but you know the closeness is gone. When you inquire, you may get innocently raised eyebrows, as if to imply you are imagining the whole thing. The irony at these times is that, although the person claims to be doing nothing, you know something is off.

Whether pointed or indirect, the cold shoulder damages the trust between people who have a connection. Instead of closeness, you feel separation and isolation. If you are a person who cares about getting along with other people, such treatment can feel like you've been sentenced to solitary confinement. Nothing you can do restores the connection with that person.

All of this is bad enough from an emotional perspective, but a cold shoulder has unseen physical effects as well. When someone turns away from you, especially an EI parent during your childhood, they are dysregulating the part of your nervous system that creates a sense of safety and support through connections with others. A cold shoulder can activate primal feelings of insecurity and even emotional collapse over losing another's approval. This loss of relational safety and emotional connection can cause stress to our major organs and blood pressure and provoke imbalance among our internal systems.

A cold shoulder makes us realize how much we need each other's goodwill. Because emotions are contagious, we each have the power to make others feel either safe or insecure. When the relationships are very close, such as between romantic partners or between parent and child, the other person's response can feel like a thumbs up or thumbs down to your very existence. For instance, if your EI parent ever turned icy and didn't want to be around you, I'm sure you remember how it depleted your life energy in both small and big ways.

What should you do if you get the cold shoulder? First, realize that the person is using behavior instead of words to express their feelings. They probably learned it in their family and are just passing it along to you. Assume, therefore, that they don't know how to talk about feelings or disagreements. But you don't have to make their shunning the centerpiece of your attention by obsessively worrying or feeling "bad." Instead, treat them as if they are unwell, saying something like: "I see that I've upset you. I wish you could talk to me about it, but maybe you can't right now. Let's talk later on when you're feeling better." Then drop it.

Just being *active* instead of passive will instantly make you feel better. The power of a cold shoulder lies in the way it shuts you down and leaves you in a passive position. When you instead respond actively with a friendly comment and then drop it, the power drains from their acting out. By seeing their behavior not as punishment but rather as their limited communication skills, you can refuse the guilt. You have correctly redefined it as a problem with emotional communication instead of a blanket rejection by the other person. The cold shoulder is the atom bomb of relationships only if you agree to accept the blame.

Do you ever give the cold shoulder? Perhaps you can try responses that are less hurtful to the relationship. How about telling the other person that you are having a hard time processing what just happened and asking for some time to sort it out? You could also make it explicit that you're not rejecting the person but do need some space. You can promise to talk about it later when things have calmed down a bit. Later, you can explain that it's just too hard to keep talking when you're really upset.

Close relationships are so full of needs and emotions that our behaviors have a big impact. We can make our corner of the world a better place when we can disagree and express hurt without withdrawing our love. When we give up the cold shoulder, we can stop punishing each other for being human and pre-serve our connections instead.

30 Such a Nice Person

Don't deny your hurt just because the other person has some good qualities.

One of the best ways we have of protecting our self-esteem is the ability to know when someone is being mean to us. If we can keep that straight, we are much less likely to blame ourselves or take unwarranted criticisms to heart. However, I find that adult children of EI parents are often reluctant to define the behavior of family members or close friends as mean or ill-intentioned. For instance, they might tell me about their distant, unloving father, then wrap up their description with a variation on the theme of "but he was a good man." Or they might cap off complaints about the thoughtless behavior of a friend with something along the lines of "but she's such a nice person."

When I hear two such contradictory things at the same time, I find myself slipping into slack-jawed incomprehension. Told two mutually exclusive things, analytical thought freezes up while the brain spins its wheels trying to do the impossible. In other words, I can't figure out how the person with the mean behavior *is* a nice person.

Thinking about confusing behavior from others, you can mesmerize yourself in the same way. To soothe the shock of being hurt by a person you like, you reassure yourself in such a way that further thought is impossible, such as "But she's a nice person" or "He's still a good guy."

I don't have a problem with generous statements about people that give them the benefit of the doubt. What I have trouble with is the way such statements are used to explain away painful, disrespectful, and rejecting behavior that would be obvious if they came from a stranger.

When you try to cover over mean and belittling behavior by calling the person "nice," "good," or "well-meaning," it hurts *your* self-esteem. It's a variation on the theme of saying that they did not mean to do it. Okay, but seeing it that way means that you may also have to conclude that you are overly sensitive or neurotic for being affected so strongly by the innocent, unintentional acts of such a "nice person."

Anytime we invalidate our own emotional reactions in order to prop up the self-image of someone else, we are setting foot on the road toward depression. This is because the truth of our own emotions is what makes us alive inside—and, I might add, aware of how other people are actually treating us.

If there are people in your life who are *both* good and bad in their behavior toward you, try letting both sides be true. You are under no moral obligation to emphasize their overall "goodness" in spite of the damage they might have caused. Don't deny the reality of your own hurt feelings just because someone has good qualities as well as bad. Accept both sides as the truth about the person and be honest to yourself about what you are dealing with. In this way, you can trust your own reactions and keep your self-esteem intact. You can still be friends with them, but that doesn't have to come at the cost of invalidating your own truth.

31 The Empty Mirror

When people don't respond to you, it can kill your spirit.

This one's for you, Mr. Tollbooth Man. Years ago, there used to be uniformed attendants at a toll plaza on the local expressway. Most of them were Zen masters of impersonal efficiency. They took your bills and gave you change, and that was that. I always made a point to say thanks, but they remained professional and poised, calmly focused on the next car. In other words, I rarely got any of them to respond to me—except one.

I remember the first time I encountered him. It was like I had been living in a dim world of candle power when suddenly his supernova smile lit up my world like a magnesium flare. This attendant leaned out of his little half-door stall and gave me the biggest, warmest smile I had ever seen. It wasn't just a smile: it was joy at the first day on the job; it was anticipation of greeting the public; it was high-quality interaction packed into two seconds. I can still remember the feeling of my own big grin when I greeted him back. *Thank goodness*, I thought, *a real human being is on the job.*

Now I realize how foolish my thought was and how wise were the other Zen-like attendants. They had found the middle way of interaction without engagement. They were survivors who had become architects of their own experience. But this joyful man dived in unprotected with no philosophy or mindful practice to buffer him against the numbing assault of unresponsive people flowing past him for hours like parts on an assembly line.

A month or two later, I passed through this man's station again, and he took my money with the saddest face and downcast eyes. Everything about him had gone out. He was gray ashes, the ruin of major depression. I never saw him again.

That bright spirit had cast his light out into the cosmos, and it had never returned. The rushing commuters probably gave little thought to his obvious desire to connect. His was a unilateral camaraderie, headed toward extinction.

A lack of response to our friendly overtures creates a unique kind of suffering. Scientists have done "still-face" experiments with mothers and babies in which the mothers look at their babies but are instructed to make no facial response to the babies' attempts to engage them. I don't have to tell you how the babies reacted; you know how it feels to get the stony face, even from a stranger, let alone your own mother. When social response is withheld, most people feel distressed, no matter what their age, and research has shown that stress hormones increase as social support is withdrawn.

Emotional connections with other people are made through mirroring each other's facial expressions and body language. These wonderful synchronies of attuned mirroring are not mystical or accidental. They are physically based and essential to healthy flourishing. The brain's mirror neurons allow us to understand another person's emotional state by reflexively mimicking their expression on our own face. This process is completely involuntary, a gift from our ancient evolutionary history.

This is why the people you spend time with are so important to your mood and mental health. We emotionally impact each other because our bodies are always copying one another.

Mirroring is the biological reason why you developed low self-esteem if you lived with an angry, critical EI parent. We cannot help but try on the other person's scowling face and disapproving look. The other person's critical attitude is not just observed. It is subliminally mimicked, countless times in countless interactions. This is the physical reason why we internalize the worst parts of EI parents and people who make us unhappy. In our interactions with them, we involuntarily mirror them over and over, one unconscious micro-expression at a time.

The tollbooth man was trying to connect in a situation where people treated social disregard as normal behavior. Warm guy that he was, he had no choice but to mirror those unresponsive faces all shift long. That's why he finally learned to look away. Whoever hired that super friendly guy should have warned him off for health reasons: this job will wreck your mirror neurons.

Keep this in mind the next time you are choosing a new job or a new friend. We usually avoid obviously negative situations, but we might not be aware of how much a lack of mirroring can hurt us. If you are lucky enough to be an emotionally engaged person, another person's blank look or lack of friendly response could be very bad for your mood and mental health.

Mr. Tollbooth Man, you were made for better things. I hope you found them.

32 Relationship Wolves

It is okay not to care about them, and it's okay to disengage from them.

There are wolves among us, as Little Red Riding Hood found out. Her mother sends her into the woods to take food to her old grandmother. A wolf stops her, and Red Riding Hood naively tells him about the grandmother's cottage. The wolf hurries off to beat her there. He swallows the grandmother whole and poses as the grandmother in bed, waiting for Red Riding Hood to appear. When she encounters the wolf wearing her grandmother's bonnet and nightgown, she hesitates and expresses her amazement at grandmother's eyes, ears, and finally teeth. Her uncertainty gives the wolf a chance to try to eat her too. But just then a woodsman hears her screams, runs to help, and dispatches the wolf, cutting open the wolf's stomach and rescuing grandma as well.

This wolf tried to nourish itself at the others' expense, and it used subterfuge to lull and confuse its victims. (I'm just a fellow traveler in the woods. I'm just a helpless invalid in bed.) The wolf's goal was to gobble up Red Riding Hood's life energy in order to replenish his own.

There are human wolves that do the same, but like Red Riding Hood, we don't see them as dangerous and so do not protect ourselves. We are not taught about the destructiveness of this kind of wolf, and so we are sitting ducks for their wiles. Relationship wolves likewise use camouflage to get their way and often present themselves as people to whom you cannot say *no*—kind of like a helpless grandmother.

These wolves are emotionally immature and masquerade as caring friends, respectable parents, or needy victims of a tragic life. Whatever their disguise, the message is the same: you have to care about me. The relationship wolf always offers the same deal: give unstintingly of your energy and attention to my needs, and I will put myself first. Relationship wolves are voracious. They are always looking for their next meal, and enough is never enough.

Relationship wolves are draining because they can't sustain a true relationship connection. Their offer of relationship is not really reciprocal, even though they may lure you in with their initial attentiveness and interest in your life. They seem to promise intimacy and bonding, but attempts to open up and truly share yourself with them land like duds. You end up feeling rushed, as if you have limited chances to slip your thoughts into the conversation. Instead of empathy, they may give you advice or switch the topic to something about them instead. You can't really connect with them in any way that is energizing, comforting, or nourishing to you. Relationship wolves are careful not to lead with their true nature. At first, relationship wolves use social seduction to present themselves as worth your fascination. What big eyes! What big ears! *All the better to focus on you, my dear!* They convince you that you are very important to them. But this is the opposite of how they are once you get involved. Those attentive eyes and ears shift and shrink as the relationship wolf devours your attention.

The secret weapon used by these stealthy wolves is the cultural norm that you should care deeply about certain people in certain roles or in certain predicaments. Victimhood, illness, or family relations are some of the trees they hide behind in order to gobble you up. They seem weak and needy, entitled to whatever they want. Your needs could never begin to approach the level of theirs. Before long, you'll find yourself thinking about them and their problems all the time. You'll find yourself feeling guilty about not giving them more attention. You'll start to dread hearing from them.

In all fairness to these wolves, we must realize they probably have been raised by wolves themselves. They likely have huge unmet dependency needs as a result.

But it is not up to you to meet these needs. It is okay not to care about them, and it's okay to disengage from them. I guarantee you they will find someone else. They convinced you that you were their only hope for getting what they needed. But that was just their greed dressed up in a bonnet and nightgown.

If the other person is not a relationship wolf, you will look forward to spending time with them. You will come away from interactions feeling happy and satisfied. Most tellingly, you'll be glad to see them next time.

Think of the woodsman. He is the type of person who is alert to other people's needs and runs forward to help. He is interested and protective and he can spot a wolf at a hundred yards. He thinks of other people and shows up when needed.

In addition to the wonderful woodsmen in the world, you have an *internal* woodsman you can call on when you get in trouble with a relationship wolf. It is that part of your personality that is strong, self-valuing, and protective of your emotional energies. This self-protective part of the personality couldn't care less if the wolf's feelings are hurt or if the wolf flies into a rage when not allowed to gobble others at will. Your inner woodsman helps keep a safe distance around you because he knows the wolf's nature.

Don't be sucked into playing the role of Red Riding Hood with a relationship wolf. Excuse yourself early and politely, before you end up in their stomach.

33　Struggling with Forgiveness

This might be asking too much of yourself.

There's a story about an anthropologist compiling a dictionary for the language of a tribe he is studying. When he gets to the word "forgiveness," he asks the tribal chief what word they use. The chief looks mystified and asks for clarification. The anthropologist explains an example of forgiveness and the chief's eyes light up. "Oh yes," he said, "Our word is *I-strike-back.*"

I love this story because it speaks truth about the thorny issue of forgiveness. You may have been taught that being a good person means to forgive, but it can be hard to do. Try as you might, you may still feel anger and lingering resentment. This is especially true if the other person doesn't seem sorry enough.

If the offending person understands your distress and deeply regrets their actions, forgiveness comes easier. You may never forget what happened, but it may shrink a little if they validate your pain and take responsibility for their part. You may change too, seeing the incident differently over time and actually developing compassion for them. Forgiveness in such cases means you lose the urge to strike back because you now see the bigger picture in which everyone involved is a fallible human being.

But what happens when people hurt you and refuse to take responsibility for it? Should you still try to forgive them? This is a common dilemma when EI people won't admit their mistakes or show empathy when they've hurt you. They lack the psychological maturity to look at themselves or realize the need for apology and restitution. Sometimes they even counterattack and blame *you*, somehow making it your fault instead. So are you still supposed to forgive them? I think this might be asking too much from yourself. And I don't think you should feel bad about not being able to do it.

Many people equate forgiveness with being a good person. But where does that leave people who find it impossible to forgive? Are you supposed to deny your true feelings and pretend you feel less hurt than you do? No, but maybe you can have all your feelings and yet not stay stuck in endless anger.

Some people argue that you should try to forgive for your own sake, not for the other person. But is this about forgiveness or letting go of obsessive anger? I think it may be possible to release anger and vengeance through constructive means, even if forgiveness is beyond you. Maybe forgiveness is something that can only come to you later, when you least expect it. Maybe we simply don't have emotional control over whether we can forgive or not in this moment. We may have to leave such things to our future development.

Meanwhile, instead of having forgiveness as your goal, what if you just decided to learn from the incident? What if you used what happened to teach you more about the kind of life you really want, the kind of people to stop wasting your time on, and how you might respond in order to avoid similar threats in the future? By making the experience useful, you might one day recognize it as a turning point in your life that made you a stronger or wiser person.

Thinking about things this way allows you to release obsessions about other people's harmful behavior. Instead of the chief's solution of *I-strike-back,* you could try a new one—neither forgiveness nor revenge—which is *I-live-forward.* You don't have to tie yourself to the past by unsuccessfully trying to forgive them; instead, you learn all you can from the experience. Give them a nod for a hard lesson that helped raise your consciousness. In this way, you turn these aggressors into catalysts for your own maturation. Through their rough help, in the form of betrayals or harm, you may start living from your authentic self more. You might find your truest values through your anger and disapproval of them. You might get clear about what you never want to be. You alone could decide to make their bad behavior show you a better way, not drag you down. Stopping at mere forgiveness could block this process. Don't settle for looking like a good person when you've got a chance to be a genuine person.

34 Don't Blame My Parents

Examining your past frees you from a predetermined future.

Sooner or later in therapy, we get to the parents. Nobody enjoys talking about them: some because they do not see the point, some because they do—and don't want to go there. It is not unusual for a person to say, "I don't want to go back and talk about all that stuff; I just want to move forward." Boy, do they have my sympathy. Who in their right mind would not prefer thinking about a fresh future to excavating the pain of the past?

It is a nuisance, but to begin, we must have the beginning. That means getting a picture of what happened to people early in life, what their parents were like, how they saw their role growing up in their family. And that's just for starters. What about the siblings, the schooling, the significant events they never forgot? Our history is a treasure trove of root causes for our lives today.

Most people do not want to go back into their past because they fear feeling guilt, anger, or low self-esteem. They hate taking all the blame themselves, but neither do they want to feel guilty for pointing a finger at their parents. It is not at all unusual to have people tell a painful story of emotional (or physical) injury by a parent and then have them quickly say, "But I don't want to blame my parents."

This reluctance to blame is understandable, especially since most people think they should leave their childhoods behind and focus on improving their futures. As a result, we shy away from the blame game. But examining your past frees you from a predetermined future.

Psychotherapy must be the only place on earth where going backward is the fastest way to move forward. Patterns of interaction in childhood teach who we are and give us deep, often unconscious expectations of what we can expect from life. Nine times out of ten, that means Mom and Dad were prime contributors to how we feel about life in the present day. Yet many people would rather not even explore that idea if they think it means blaming their parents.

But here is another way to look at it, one that will make you less guilty about examining your parents' roles. The goal in good therapy is not to assign blame and stop there. It is not blame we are after; it is truth. Whoever said that the truth shall set you free would probably be in favor of a productive therapy session or two. The goal is to see both you and your parents as fallible human beings, with enough psychological injuries on both sides to sink a battleship. You are looking not to disparage your parents but to accept them as the limited human beings they most assuredly were. Then you can see something important: how their limitations affected your view of yourself and your world.

Just like babies, parents signal their distress through alarming behavior, getting us to feel as upset as they are. Neither babies nor parents are maliciously striving to make life miserable for others; they are just expressing their pain in the only way they know how. When we look back in therapy at how our parents acted, it's like attempting to decipher a coded language. We're trying to figure out what psychological issues they were stuck in through the way they treated us.

When a person gains an insight into his or her parent's deeper motivations and unresolved problems, there is a click of new awareness. Suddenly, years of interaction with that parent are seen in a new light. Pain that had been unconsciously passed down from one generation to another now has a name. Pain that had seemed senseless now has a cause. We were hurt not because we are bad people or our parents were bad people. It happened because the generations before us lacked a science with which to mitigate the costs of unattended emotional pain.

Through the process of psychotherapy, we have a chance to finally understand and put into words what might have been driving our family's pain for generations.

Is this blaming our parents? Hardly. It is more as if we are *expressing* our parents. Through our self-understanding, we are translating their unspoken needs in ways they could not. We ought to be jumping at the chance to figure out our relationship with them so that we do not have to pass along untranslated pain to our children. Our parents might not have been able to figure it out in their lives and times. Their only option was to pass along their pain in silent hopes it might be deciphered by someone later. That family code breaker might turn out to be you.

35 Meeting Your Maker

When we go home to family, we are returning to the sculptor's atelier.

Family is the raw stone out of which we were sculpted. Michelangelo said the secret of sculpting his masterpiece *David* was simply to remove everything that wasn't *David*. The beauty of *David* was inside the stone all along but had to be brought out by the strikes of Michelangelo's chisel.

We too start out as largely raw material, our individuality unformed. Then, as we interact with family members, the chiseling begins, and the extraneous pieces start falling away. Our true self begins to reveal its curves and corners as we emerge from the raw matrix of family relationships. In large part, we discover ourselves through the difficult interactions that tell us who we are not.

We might have reinvented ourselves outside the family, but going home takes us back to the beginnings of who we were before we had the choice to be whatever we wanted. Going home for visits can remind us of how challenging those beginnings might have been. But if we hadn't had someone to resist and resent along the way, would we ever have uncovered our true individuality? We may wish we had been treated with more care, but the creation of a strong and resilient soul often seems to emerge from the brutish business of conflict with a loved one.

When we go home to family, even an EI family, we are returning to the sculptor's atelier. Here is where we found our form. All the miseries of childhood were the processes by which large chunks of marble were cracked away to reveal our roughened shape, while the joys of childhood were the experiences by which we were lovingly polished into a unique expression of humanity. We couldn't have become who we are today without the stress of being hammered and sanded by an abundance of friction. If we were lucky, by the time we got out of the family to start our own life, we emerged as solid as *David*, so toughened by the creative work that we were ready to take on Goliaths.

Returning to family can be stressful because we are reminded of our struggles to grow up. Without our differences—like the strikes of iron against marble—we might have remained so much a part of the family that we would not have had our own lives. Perhaps you know someone who has experienced this: the stone was left as it was and thus remained unformed and uncreated. There just wasn't enough friction with the parent to bring the true individual into being.

But returning home also gives us the reassurance of tradition. No matter what we have accomplished in our lives, it's nice to have some things remain the same. For good or bad, familiarity has its comforts. When we return to family, we are returning to our source, the quarry from which we were hewn.

Maybe it would drive us crazy to live there again, but the sensation of reentering the family can be a relief to the child in us. Back we go into the marble mountain, where we are once more an amalgamized bit of the whole, no longer separate or special. Some early part of us seems to welcome this swallowing up, this smudging of the lines that define us as separate individuals. Returning to family can offer a giving-in to gravity after the long struggle to make it on our own, like the baby tired of standing who plops its bottom back on the floor with satisfaction.

Family gatherings can feel like a chance to emotionally regress after the long push forward of adult life. We could embrace this as a desirable process. Instead of the unending drive to make something of ourselves and take responsibility for our failings, within our family, we can just let go and blame them for our frustrations. It's a delicious indulgence after making it on our own for so long. We can go home and react inside like children again. Within our original family, we are freed from our role as adults, and we get to sample the old resentments and hurt feelings that fired our desire to self-create in the first place.

So what should our response be when we return to the family workshop where we were sculpted?

Let's imagine how *David* and Michelangelo handled it. I wonder what *David* had to say to Michelangelo once he was fully finished and brought into this world. Might he have said to his creator, "Did it have to be so painful?" Perhaps he would say, "Surely there was another way to get me out of that stone without so much conflict and pounding?" Or would he let all that go, standing there gleaming from all the friction, a beautifully burnished magnificence that had withstood the swing of his maker's mallet. Maybe he would just say, "Thank you. It was worth it all just to be here."

How It Feels to Be
Treated Well

Growing up subject to others' emotional immaturity can be frustrating and emotionally painful. Consequently, you may feel especially grateful when delightful people come along to make you feel like all is right with the world. Around them, it feels natural to be yourself. Your thinking is clear, your heart feels warm, and they draw the very best out of you. You simultaneously become more yourself—and more than yourself.

36   What Mr. Rogers Loved in You

Mr. Rogers reminds us that what happens inside us is just as important as what happens outside us.

Thank goodness for Fred Rogers. Mr. Rogers kept his attention on true feelings. He never lost sight of that four-year-old inside each of us.

Mr. Rogers made us believe that the inside of us was enough for him. Just by virtue of having drawn a breath, you were special and lovable. You were *so* special, in fact, he wanted to know *would* you be his and *could* you be his, because he always wanted *to live in a neighborhood with you.* Listen to those lyrics. It's a valentine sung from someone who knows what love really is.

Mr. Rogers was different from your EI parent and many of the people you know because he welcomed *all* the parts of you in his neighborhood. He stated there was always room for you, your anger, and your hurt feelings too. One of his little songs asked, "What do you do with the bad you feel, when you feel so bad you could bite?" When was the last time someone showed you that kind of interest, especially when you were angry and hurt? Mr. Rogers reminds us that what happens inside us is just as important as what happens outside us.

Mr. Rogers was an existentialist, and he came right down on the side of everyone's right to be here. He taught that just being here *is* your meaning. You don't have to prove anything, achieve something, or otherwise wow the people around you in order to be worthy of love. All you have to do is be alive. And his audiences knew from listening to how he talked that he had thought this all out. He was not a blithe or superficial sort of man. No, he had solid reasons for what he was doing. Mr. Rogers knew that once you were a four-year-old in need of love and safety, you were always, at some level, a four-year-old in need of love and safety.

The best relationships, if you think about it, all have Mr. Rogers's brand of existentialism in them. The greatest gift you can be given is to know that someone cherishes your presence in the world. We all need to be around people for whom our very existence is a delight. That's the kind of love that does not see you as a role or a function but as a fascinating, vital being who exists to enjoy and be enjoyed. Mr. Rogers understood this totally.

Mr. Rogers's programs continue to mesmerize us, even as the action-addicted synapses in our brains are tempted to scream at his easygoing pace. But if you listen to him for a few minutes, the deep emotional centers of your brain start unspooling in long coils of relaxation. *Aah…Mr. Rogers says all you have to do is be.* You are special whether you accomplish anything or not. He says you are worthy of care even when you are bad or angry. You have a good reason for all your feelings, he tells you, and he knows how hard you try. He is not ambitious for you nor critical of you. He likes you just the way you are, whether you are four or forty.

We may not be four years old anymore, but our emotional needs are exactly the same. We want someone to light up when we come in the room, and we don't want to be forgotten about when we are apart. We want to be forgiven when we are bad, and we want someone to put us first. We want someone to feel sad when we are hurt, not just say the right thing. We want someone to pay close attention when we are scared and need to talk. We want someone to be preoccupied with our security and well-being. Most of all, we want to have an effect on others, to have them treat us like we are really alive and as real as real can be. Maybe that's the sum of what Fred Rogers came to tell us, to treat one another like every one of us is really alive inside. That's the way to keep on loving each other, even when we feel bad enough to bite.

37 The Dalai Lama Wants You to Be Happy

Happiness is a pursuit best aided by a scientific devotion to self-knowledge.

Once I had the privilege of attending a teaching given by the Dalai Lama. As the spiritual leader of Tibetan Buddhism, he spoke at American University to a full house. As I entered the arena, looking for my seat in the bleachers, I was stopped short by the stage backdrop set up for the Dalai Lama. It was a gorgeous, huge silk wall-hanging—approximately three stories high and nearly as wide—of a magnificent golden yellow Buddha, replete with lotuses and intricate designs of every possible hue.

Directly beneath this enormous image was the Dalai Lama's throne, set on a richly carpeted, raised dais. Filling the lower stage, left and right, were Buddhist monks and nuns, sitting cross-legged, their maroon and saffron robes adding to the colorful majesty of the scene.

When the Dalai Lama approached the stage from the right of the arena, you could feel the hush of the crowd. There he was in his trademarked horn-rimmed spectacles, slightly stooped, his bare right arm reaching out from his robe to touch and greet people. It was clear from his stops all along the way that he perceived each person as a single destination. There were no strides toward the stage or big waves to the anonymous crowd; there was individual contact after individual contact.

Once on stage, he greeted all the monks and nuns in similar fashion, sent bowed greetings and blessings into all sections of the crowd—seeming to smile at individuals—and then prostrated himself several times before the Buddha. With careful assistance from his aides, he finally ascended to his chair, removed his shoes, and arranged himself comfortably in the lotus position. After introductions, he chatted amiably with the crowd, interrupting himself at one point with a loud sneeze, which he said serves him well when audiences get sleepy. His laughter was irrepressible and delighted.

While I was interested in what His Holiness might have to teach me about Buddhism, I was not prepared for how deeply psychological his philosophy was. Indeed, rather than gaining spiritual enlightenment, I was frantically taking notes for my clinical practice. It seems the Dalai Lama and I in some ways may be in the same line of work.

Buddhism has a couple of thousand years on clinical psychology, but some of its tenets are so modern it could easily be one of the new positive psychologies sweeping the fields of psychotherapy and neuroscience. For centuries before Christianity, Buddhism promoted the idea that our thoughts make up our emotional reality and that the bulk of our suffering comes from clinging to painful beliefs that exhaust and hurt us. According to Buddhism, in order to free ourselves from needless suffering, we must investigate our rigid beliefs and seek compassion for both ourselves and other people.

I agree that we are not suffering because we are bad; we are suffering because we are deluded. Under the tyranny of ego attachments, we think our worth lies in things and social status. We indulge in extreme and harsh judgments. We mistakenly believe the cause for our misery lies in the outside world rather than realizing the damage is caused by our own thinking. Modern psychology warns against the same delusions.

Perhaps the Dalai Lama's most radical idea can be found in his book *The Art of Happiness*. The first line in this book declares that the purpose of our life is to seek happiness. He explains that happiness is a pursuit best aided by a scientific devotion to self-knowledge. It is up to each of us to investigate what our thoughts do to our equilibrium. The trick is to gradually eliminate those factors that make us unhappy while deliberately cultivating those that nourish us.

Both psychology and the Dalai Lama say that our happiness is determined by our state of mind and that the best way to improve our state of mind is through learning. By educating ourselves about how our minds work, we can stop our thoughts from luring us into fear and unhappiness. Modern-day psychotherapy does exactly the same thing, teaching people how to monitor their own thoughts and beliefs so that they can more consciously direct their mood and outlook. Both Tibetan Buddhism and cognitive therapy challenge distorted thinking and extreme beliefs, especially those all-or-nothing thoughts that make us feel inadequate or unworthy.

As the Dalai Lama was finishing his teaching from his magnificent throne that day, he shielded his eyes from the bright lights by slipping on a visor cap in a perfectly matching shade of maroon. The crowd burst into laughter seeing His Holiness looking ready for a day at the ballpark, and he laughed too, saying, "I don't care. It's practical!"

There was the Dalai Lama's advice about life in a nutshell: Use what makes you feel better, and don't let appearances get in the way. Buddha himself could not have said it better.

38 Kindness Lessons from a Dentist

I got to stay a person; I didn't have to turn into a patient.

My dentist is going to retire one of these days, and I'm trying to figure out how to follow him home. Will I miss getting my teeth worked on? Do I have fond feelings for the whir of the drill? Far from it. My childhood dentist filled a few cavities without Novocain, so I have a legitimate fear of dentists.

But years ago, I found my dentist, Jules, and it was the beginning of dental trust. When working on a hard-to-get-to tooth recently, Jules apologized for having me in such a firm headlock. "Just trying to keep your head steady," he explained. I couldn't respond because my mouth was holding an array of implements like an open suitcase. But what I wanted to tell him was that the firm pressure was weirdly comforting, the dental version of the rescue hold. I did not feel restrained; I felt secure.

Jules's most obvious skills were in his dexterous hands, but he was truly gifted in the knack of getting along with people. For long-term success, it is not enough to know your trade; you have to be aware of your trade's effect on others.

Jules's instinct for human connection gave him a way with people. He was both sensitive and in command. He might chat me up like the consummate gentleman he was, but once he initiated my dental exam, I was perfectly willing to put him in charge. Emotional connection leads to trust. I wasn't just his patient; I felt like his pet project.

Anyone going to see an expert is usually nervous and in a one-down position. The situation is ripe for professionals to capitalize on the power offered to them. They get to play the expert, the one who knows everything—perhaps like an EI parent. But too often, professionals and parents lose sight of the person as they focus on the problem. Jules taught me that anyone, including a dentist, can be an expert in humanity above all.

For example, once when Jules was on vacation, I had to get a tooth looked at by a different dentist. I knew I was in trouble when the dentist's eyes lit up as I described my problem. "Ooh…that's not good!" was her dreadful response. The unmistakable relish in her tone was alarming, and I decided to wait for Jules to get back.

Now, Jules would never make such a beginner's mistake like getting your patient frightened *before* you started working on her. He had a whole bag of tricks (emotionally intelligent responses) designed to make his patients feel hopeful and accepting about whatever had to happen next. I recommend the following behaviors to any health professional.

He praised his patients' strengths. "You keep a beautiful mouth, dear!" Jules would say, with the appreciation a jeweler shows for fine stones. "I wish everyone took care of their teeth like you do." Jules was also fond of muttering, "Perfect…perfect!" as he checked my teeth. It's hard to be scared when you're feeling proud. He looked for problems, but he remarked on strengths.

He didn't scare his patients with careless imagery. Jules was careful about how he put things. He would never use a scary metaphor like "decay could be lurking," as one unenlightened hygienist put it. Jules would just size up the situation, tell you what needed to be done, and make the job sound like simple home maintenance: "We're just going to clean it out, seal it up, and you'll have many years of good use from this."

When checking mouth tissues, the worse thing Jules ever said was, "You may now stick your tongue out at me," a rather empowering instruction if you think about it. Never in a million years would he raise the specter of disease like a different dentist once did: "Now I'm going to check you for mouth cancer." (Whoa…I'm feeling worse, Doc!)

He hid the needles. I used to think Jules must keep his anesthetizing needles in his left armpit. Right before I closed my eyes, I would catch a glimpse of him reaching back between his left side and arm. (I stopped looking at that point.) Later I asked his assistant where *did* he keep those needles, and she said, "Oh, I stand behind him and put the needle in his hand when he reaches back." This was empathy incarnate, mercy in action, and wisdom in practice. Please, people, no waving about of scary implements.

He gave me hope we would soon be done. No fan of protracting suspense, Jules would announce each step in the process with a simple "Now we're going to…" soon followed by "Almost done…Just finishing up a bit…You'll be out of here soon…Excellent! Perfect!" It probably took longer than he made it seem, but for most procedures, he convinced me I was right around the corner from freedom.

Jules's manner always made me feel like I was more than the state of my teeth. He asked about my family and shared stories; he treated me as a whole person first and a set of teeth second. I got to stay a *person*; I didn't have to turn into a *patient*. I am much stronger when I am treated like a person and much weaker when I am treated like a patient. For all the years I have known this dentist, I have walked in there a human being and stayed a human being. Of course, I was always relieved to leave his office, but always giddy with relief that he made it so pleasant.

I'm sure most professionals who emphasize their expert role are just trying to inspire confidence. But believe me, by the time a person enters an exam room, that person has gotten the message about the expert thing. At that point, they need calming down, not being talked down to.

The day is coming when medical professionals will learn these people skills right up there with anatomy and ethics, and if there is anything to the mind–body connection, it will do their customers good. Until then, we could all use more of my good dentist's style and we could all apply it better. How would it feel if everyone were treated this way?

Perfect, perfect.

39 Finding a Spiritual Teacher

*Wise and trustworthy guides will urge you to develop your own
potential instead of expecting your adoration.*

A spiritual seeker heard about a guru on the far side of the world who had the
secret to the meaning of life. Though this sage lived in a cave high atop a
remote mountain, the seeker set off to find him at all costs. Enduring unimagi-
nable hardships for years, following many false leads, the seeker finally found
and scaled the perilous mountain to the guru's cave. Exhausted after the climb,
the seeker crawled to the guru who sat cross-legged on a large boulder in front
of his rocky cave.

"Oh Master," the seeker panted, "tell me please. What is the secret of life?"

The guru smiled down at the seeker. After a long pause, he said, "Life is
like a fountain."

The seeker blinked at him for several moments. "Life is like a fountain?"
asked the seeker incredulously.

The guru hesitated. Then he slowly said, "You mean, life *isn't* like a
fountain?"

The moral of this story is to never fear questioning your spiritual heroes.
We all have an innate tendency to find someone to idealize, someone we can
relate to as a superior being. But we often project special qualities onto other
people because we don't believe we could be that wise ourselves. Instead of
nurturing our own growth, it can feel more natural to pin our hopes onto an
idealized master. Too often, we fall for self-styled stars who need to be looked
up to rather than ethical guides who teach us how to develop ourselves.

Many of us do this because we were raised to defer to authority and creden-
tials no matter what, suppressing our doubts whenever an authority—especially
an EI parent—made a questionable pronouncement. We take it for granted

that experts know best, especially in the spiritual realm. It feels reassuring to put ourselves in the hands of people who show no self-doubt, who seem absolutely confident about their beliefs. But you have to be careful that you're not putting yourself in the hands of a narcissist who needs to be more important than anyone else.

If anything is true in this world, it is that wise and trustworthy guides will urge you to develop your own potential instead of expecting your adoration. They will educate and encourage you, not recruit you as their acolyte. Wise guides enjoy explaining things and answering tough questions because they welcome the chance to think more deeply about their beliefs. If you feel baffled, they'll keep looking for ways to make things clearer. They won't muddy your inquiries with vague platitudes or mysterious evasions. They don't hide behind obfuscation or promises to reveal the truth once you've paid up.

In contrast, self-glorifying spiritual teachers will make you feel embarrassed for putting them on the spot. They expect their clichés to stay airtight and unquestioned. It feels impolite to even notice that their wisdom doesn't quite add up.

There's a difference between feeling awe and feeling confusion. We all have a little awe-center in us that recognizes real wisdom and admirable character in another person. We naturally trust them and sense they won't treat our ignorance with contempt. But for narcissistic spiritual leaders, confusion and unquestioning obedience are their stock and trade. Their power comes from getting you to renounce your doubts and trust they know better than you. They imply you are being small-minded if you hold them to the same moral and fair-minded standards that the rest of us follow.

Untrustworthy teachers also show contradictions between what they preach and how they behave. You can't get their behavior and beliefs to go together. They are neither self-reflective nor self-aware when it comes to their impulses, and, therefore, they don't see it when they promote one set of standards yet live by another. They never notice the illogic of saying one thing and doing the exact opposite. They are like those Möbius strips, optical illusion drawings that show a peculiar effect—when you follow a picture's line with your eyes, it suddenly disappears and turns into something else.

When you find genuine and trustworthy life teachers, you may not be able to get your head around everything they say, but a deeper part of yourself feels safe and cared for by them, even if you can't articulate it. Your questions are not only accepted but also encouraged and enjoyed.

Let's return now to our original story. Hats off to that guru who had the humility to question his revelation. But what if the seeker had simply worshipped the guru and went forth passing along the wisdom that life is like a fountain? What if the seeker had suppressed doubts by telling subsequent followers that many years of meditation, prayer, and donations would be needed to truly understand this great awareness? Thankfully, our seeker had an honest reaction and wondered aloud if the guru knew what he was talking about. It's good to keep in mind that people who give you the feeling that there's something wrong with you when you question them are offering a cult of personality, not a pathway to truth.

40   Pets Who Love Us

We are made for unconditional love, from start to finish.

Thank goodness for pets. Since we can't have psychotherapists in every home, our precious friends from the animal kingdom must do double duty to keep us sane. Actually, animals do a much better job than clinicians could ever hope to. And until therapists learn to leap up with joy at the arrival of their clients while lavishing unrestrained adoration on their very being, they will always be a distant second to pets.

Plenty of research has come out on the positive emotional and physical effects of interactions with friendly animals. If pets can lower the blood pressure of someone in a hospital bed, imagine what they can do for you at the end of every day. What is it about these critters that we respond to so deeply?

It is their brains. Ounce for ounce, domesticated mammal pets have spent nearly their whole neuronal allowance on the emotional bonding centers of the brain. Neurologically speaking, they are little love machines. Actually, they are little *unconditional* love machines.

All mammal brains are made up of three major parts, each quite neurologically distinct. The neocortex is the thinking part that surrounds the emotional centers, which in turn sit atop the source of our survival instincts. The thinking part of the brain is given short shrift in your cat and is only a little more developed in your dog. They really don't need much of it to find their food and raise their families. But compared to other mammals, human beings have plunked down most of their genetic inheritance on their huge neocortex, with powerful results. The human thinking brain has worked well enough to take over the world.

But who needs the world when you come home after a long day or when your partner, teenager, or two-year-old is giving you a hard time? We don't want the world at that point; we want fur and affection. We crave a sympathetic cuddle.

In their book *A General Theory of Love*, psychiatrists Thomas Lewis, Fari Amini, and Richard Lannon have figured out why this is so. This review of the studies on attachment and emotional connection stresses the mental and physical importance of having emotional bonds with other mammals. It is a plus if these receptive mammals turn out to be the humans in your life, but a dog will do.

Their theory (backed up by plenty of research in the field) is that mammals share an almost mystical resonance between the emotional parts of their brains, which is why we can easily sense another's feelings. Picking up your loved one's bad mood or getting swept away by mob frenzies are examples of your emotional system communicating quickly and directly with other mammal brains, like tuning instantaneously in to the same radio station.

This natural resonance, this mutual echoing between brains, keeps us in sync with each other. We need this brain-harmonizing to regulate not only our emotional well-being but our physical health as well. When one emotional brain finds another emotional brain willing to lick its face, figuratively speaking, the whole organism feels stabilized and steadied. We feel less lost, less confused. Stress resistance goes up, thinking is clearer, and immune function is improved. Babies especially count on Mom's attentiveness to stabilize them emotionally and physically. Such devoted attunement is crucial for the human infant to thrive and even survive. We are made for unconditional love, from start to finish.

What many unhappy childhoods and marriages have in common is an inability to achieve emotional resonance when it counts. For instance, when we crave bonding and full attention, the other person's thinking brain just won't do. In fact, if someone responds to our *emotional* need for connection with a *thinking* response (such as advice or problem-solving), we feel unseen and slighted. Your pet would never make such an egregious social error.

The love of a pet has seen many a person through a dark night of the soul. And when a pet dies, we all know how much of our heart they take with them. As far as the loving part of our brain is concerned, a mammal is a mammal, and that's all that matters. The connection between a person and pet is one of the last bastions of unconditional love still available to us all. It's the best part of mother love, all over again.

Emotionally Mature Parenting

When it's your turn to be the parent, sometimes you try new ways and other times you fall back into what you grew up with. But your overarching goal is to help your children mature into strong, capable, and authentic people capable of rewarding relationships. Your own emotional maturation will help you give your children what they need: to have some predictable structure, to be seen for who they are, to be treated with tact, and ultimately to be set free with a blessing. Rather than struggle against children's developmental stages (or your own as a parent), you can use the natural tides of change to swim further toward who you really are.

41 The Truth about Children

Children are just as full of human nature as we are.

The truth about children is that they are here to meet their needs, not ours. Some parents don't realize this and think that children should be willing to act against their self-interest, give up what they want most, and do whatever a parent asks. For people who grew up with EI parents, this may be the model they're most familiar with. When the child refuses or sneaks around the rules, such parents feel betrayed. The child's disobedience makes it seem like the child does not really love them. But this is not about love; it is about the power differential that causes any subordinate to acquiesce to people who have power over them while plotting a way around them. Children are just as full of human nature as we are.

Children test every bit of your resolve to be a good person. They push your buttons and are so staggeringly egocentric it can take your breath away. High points for selfish behavior are especially vivid in the six-year-old, the thirteen-year-old, and the college freshman. Sometimes it seems like they expect full support while simultaneously demanding you pretend you don't exist. That can be hard to take as a parent.

Parents who were overcontrolled by their own EI parents might see their children's normal limit-testing as disrespect or even defiance. Instead of understanding that a kid will naturally try to get what he or she wants, it is seen as a rebellion against your authority.

But no healthy child wants to overthrow a parent. Where would he or she be then? Children are just normal human beings with healthy self-interest, and they are never going to accept restraint or frustration without protest. You can learn to take these behaviors as understandable reactions instead of a challenge to authority.

Parents always hold the strategic advantage over a kid. Children are just not that complicated. They are lousy at long-range strategy. They react very predictably. They have simple buttons you can push and pretty much get what you want. But you have to be smart about it and use what works. Good parenting books can tell you all the ways you can work with a child's simple motives and ultimately win their cooperation. I say "ultimately" because nothing is instant in child-rearing: it is all about repetition, repetition, repetition.

If parents expect a child to have the reasoning skills and frustration tolerance of an adult, they will create anger or withdrawal instead of compliance. When parents try to enforce instant capitulation from a child, whether through coercion or guilt, they usually get blowback instead. Worse, sometimes the child will not fight back overtly but will slide into passive-aggressive disengagement where the parents have no power at all.

Children need just a few things. Children want the same regard from their parents that is found between equal adults. They don't need the same rights or permissions, but they do need to be treated with consideration. If they get that, they ultimately (there's that word again) will turn into nice people who can see your point occasionally. But you, the parent, need to be prepared to wait a long time to see some sign of good judgment and responsibility in them. The awful truth is that children just need you to have unearthly unconditional love with zero needs for affirmation or validation from them. They need you to be patient while they mature and develop responsibility, and they need you to tolerate enough of their mistakes and selfish behaviors to make your jaw drop.

In return, your kids will do something important for you as well. They'll make you revisit your past. Maybe they have come into your life to stir up your old childhood issues, maybe with an EI parent, for one last look-see. The truth about children is that they bring your own childhood back. When they push your buttons, they are always hitting replay. Your children's blatant egocentrism will trigger the times where you have felt devalued or disrespected in your life. Your kids give you a chance to finally deal with old hurt feelings and allow you to process them and make them a part of your history, not an ongoing part of your present. Maybe those buttons they are pushing have been the right ones all along, the ones that could help you grow.

42 Best-Kept Secret in Parenting

Like all human beings, children crave respect.

The best-kept secret in parenting is that children respond to exactly the same treatment that works with adults. There are not different standards for what works with kids and what works with grown-ups. It is all pretty much the same set of rules. People of all ages like to be treated like intelligent, sentient beings instead of underlings.

Children love it when parents take them seriously and recognize them as real people with their own tastes. Like all human beings, children crave respect. They like to know why they are doing things, and they balk at demands for unquestioning obedience.

Adults react the exact same way. Just think about the good and bad bosses you have had. Nobody likes to work for a harsh, sarcastic boss who orders people around and does not explain why decisions were made. But a boss who treats employees with respect is likely to gain appreciation and devotion over time. Then, when that good boss needs to ask for the extra mile, the employees want to give it because they have been treated well.

Good bosses and good parents use the same approach with the same results: their employees and children like to be around them. It is hard to have real influence when others want to keep their distance from you. When parents are angry and blaming, children stop listening to what the parents are saying and concentrate instead on escaping from the unpleasantness—which you may recognize from your own childhood experiences. On the other hand, being treated with patience and reason is an inherently positive experience, and children will usually take correction pretty well if the adults do not attack their dignity.

Some parents, especially EI ones, act like courtesy is only for grown-ups. We would never dream of controlling our friends in the kind of high-handed way we use with our children. We probably wouldn't threaten our friends to comply or else, and we wouldn't announce we are all leaving right now without asking if they were ready. We would not remind our friends repeatedly of what they had not done right, nor would we withhold our love from them until they did what we wanted. We wouldn't do these things partly because we know our friends would probably leave us if we treated them that way.

Instead of speaking to children in a way that invites collaboration (good boss approach), many parents give children commands, even when it's not necessary, and routinely hang the threat of punishment over their heads (bad boss approach). Many of us have been taught that this is what it means to be a strong, authoritative parent. We think this will be good for our children in the long run. But what can be effective about making our children want to get away from us?

Children do not automatically run wild if their parents treat them with consideration and courtesy. Just like adults, children like rules and routines—if the rules make sense and do not seem arbitrary. Children have consciences, and after some face-saving protests, they are usually willing to accept consequences if they are fairly administered. As adults, we still have plenty of natural authority due to our wisdom and experience, and children know this. They want to be protected by our adult good sense, and most of them will not launch into major rebellion when our limits are fair and appropriate to their age.

Don't forget this secret to great parenting: children are real people on the inside, just like you and me. They gravitate to people who believe the best of them, give them time to learn, and do not repeatedly remind them of their mistakes and shortcomings. People of all ages like to be asked, not told. They appreciate it when their needs are taken into consideration. Whether it is with a child or an adult, happy living always comes down to how well we can get other people to want to cooperate with us.

43   Focus Your Praise

Think of praise as a very bright light you are wielding.

Recently I had the opportunity to watch an exuberant mother heap praise upon her child who had just managed the musical equivalent of a slam dunk at her piano recital. "I am so *proud* of you!" the jubilant mom said over and over.

In an embarrassed lowered voice, the daughter groaned, "*Mom...*," as she tucked her head and shifted her eyes around to see who might be listening.

Now, there was no question in my mind that this happy mother meant no harm. She was trying to do all the right things: reinforcing her daughter's self-esteem, recognizing her skill, and celebrating her success. Her parenting theory seemed to be "The more praise, the better." Yet it was clear the child just wanted her to stop.

Did this girl have low self-esteem? Was she unable to think positively about herself? It did not seem that way. I mean, the kid was beaming when she came offstage. She knew she had aced it. What seemed to be making her uncomfortable was more about the *way* the mom was praising her.

The incident reminded me of someone shining a powerful flashlight directly in someone's eyes, saying, "There! Now you can see better." True, light does help us to see better, but to be useful, it must be indirect and focused on the thing we need to see, not flooding our retinas with painful glare. That is the way praise is. Think of it as a very bright light you are wielding, and you will know exactly how to handle it. You shine it on what the person has done and talk about *that*.

This approach would have enabled that mother to stand beside her daughter, shining the light of praise, while together they both enjoyed admiring her performance. For instance, instead of saying "I'm so proud of you!" the mom might have said something about the performance itself, like "That was masterful!" or "The way you played that one part brought tears to my eyes!" or "What a *beautiful* piece of work you did!" It sounds like a subtle difference, but it is not. The language we use is intended to paint specific pictures in our minds.

What kind of picture do you get when you hear "I'm so proud of you"? I see a beaming parent standing *over* a small child bestowing approval while the child passively absorbs the parent's judgment. But when the child's performance or achievement ("What a topnotch job!") is the focus, I see the parent standing *beside* the child, with an arm around the shoulders, while they both look at the child's achievement agreeing that it was pretty darned good.

You see, one kind of praise focuses on the parent's pride and the other focuses on the quality of the child's achievement. When the praise is centered just on the parent's pride, there can be a little uneasiness involved in being the recipient. Emphasizing parental pride might also imply the unspoken message "this time," as in "I am so proud of you *this time.*" It reminds me of those bumper stickers displaying My *child is an honor roll student.* What happens if the child doesn't make it the next grading period? Will you still be proud of the child then?

On the other hand, when you praise the *performance,* there is no pressure. It is done, they did a great job, and nobody can ever take it away from them. Plus the emphasis is on what the *child* did well, not on making the parent proud. Praising the accomplishment prepares the way for more achievement, but expressing pride emphasizes parental approval.

When you concentrate on appreciating and enjoying what your child accomplished, then both of you can join in the emotional closeness of celebrating a job well done. This is a strengthening experience, helping the child see that doing well results in communal appreciation. Parental expressions of pride make a child feel special, to be sure, but sometimes a little uncomfortable, a little in danger of falling off the pedestal.

This approach holds for employees, spouses, and anyone else whose performance you respond to. Think back to any award banquet you have ever attended. Award presenters talk about what the recipient did. They do not just say, "I'm so proud of you!" and hand them the award. Recognition is about taking the time to cite the facts, not just expressing our happy feelings.

Lest you think I am a purist in this matter, let me hurry to say that there are plenty of times when a straight, simple "I am so proud of you!" cannot be denied and springs from our lips no matter what. Sometimes it really is the only thing to say because it comes from the heart so honestly. I am just suggesting that we quickly turn the light back onto the other person's achievement rather than our own proud reactions. Then praise is much easier to take.

44 How to Comfort an Extrovert

Try not to take their statements too personally nor their reactions too literally.

Extrovert kids have a hard time putting up with a dull moment, and that goes for their emotional life as well. When an extroverted child becomes upset, any kind of problem easily turns into a call to arms. Extroverts instinctively look outside themselves to find relief when they are distressed. The more introverted approach of thinking out a problem is an alien concept to the agitated extrovert mind. Action feels right to them, and they have found that doing something—anything—makes them feel better immediately.

There are three things that extroverted children tend to do when upset: they exaggerate the situation and their reactions to it; they project blame; and they threaten drastic action. Knowing how to respond to these extroverted reactions can mean the difference between helping and making things worse.

First of all, it is important not to take every exaggerated thing that the extrovert says in a moment of anger or hurt seriously. Exaggeration comes naturally to the bighearted extrovert anyway, and that tendency becomes amplified when they are upset. In the heat of the moment, extroverts can blurt out things that stick in their loved one's mind like an arrow. Did they mean it? Maybe not, but you can bet that they said it with vehemence.

Later, however, when the moment has passed, the extrovert may dismiss what he or she said and wonder why other people are still so upset. In the extrovert's mind, it was just blowing off steam. Many extroverts have been genuinely surprised that other people are still feeling the effect of their hot words long after the incident has faded for the extrovert.

One way to understand an extrovert's magnified reactions is to see them as emotional attempts to seek a connection when they are distressed. Emotional hurts or unsolved problems make extroverted kids feel lonely and isolated— one of the most painful states an extrovert can be in. The extrovert's agitated behavior when things are not going well shows how isolated they feel. They desperately need to connect with another person at these times.

Upset extroverts also try to make themselves feel better by blaming others and threatening drastic action. Forget about self-examination and emotional reflection—the initial way extroverts feel better is by imagining action that gets their power back. Trying to get extroverts to stop blaming and be fair when they are upset will only result in a mutual bout of frustration. They need to blame until they calm down enough to see things differently. It is pointless to argue with them when they are upset since blaming is their natural, outward way of releasing hurt. Later on, when things have cooled down and the extrovert feels safe again, you can return to the discussion with another point of view, and then your extroverted child may be able to hear you.

Deeply involved interaction and intense, responsive listening are the greatest comforts you can offer extroverts. Try not to take their statements too personally nor their reactions too literally. Focus on their feelings and unmet needs instead of what they may be threatening to do. Just remember that when extroverts talk of action and blaming, they are really asking for your understanding and loads of sympathetic comments. Listen past the bluster and blame to get to the fear underneath. Freely exaggerate your empathic responses, reflecting their emotional distress fully.

Extroverts in pain desperately want to unburden themselves into your receptive heart. Even if they are saying crazy things, extroverts are just trying to communicate the emotion as vividly as possible. To comfort them, listen with your heart—not your mind—to the pain, fear, or disappointment underneath, and give lots of clear signals that you are hearing them.

Once extroverted children feel that you have responded vigorously to their feelings, they will feel strangely satisfied and calmed. The more you accept and reflect their distress unconditionally, the more easily they can let go and calm down—but only after they know that you joined them in their deepest place of hurt. Anything less makes them continue to feel isolated and desperate for relief. The more you convince them that you accept and understand their distress, the faster you will see them return to their naturally upbeat nature.

45 How to Comfort an Introvert

The introvert is secretly hoping the other person does not give up.

There are two types of children in the world: the ones who demand comforting and the ones who hide from it. Extroverts are the expressive ones, broadcasting their distress openly, whether in words or actions. When they are upset, their emotions quickly transform into some kind of interaction with other people. An extroverted child's pain may come out in the form of misbehavior or anger because extroverts cannot help but engage other people when they are hurting. Introverts are quite the opposite.

When introverted children get upset, they instinctively hide their feelings and *avoid* interaction. In contrast to the extroverts' urge to turn outward with their distress, the introvert is like the sea anemone, sucking itself back into its inner world at the first sign of pain. This withdrawal instinct is designed to form an impenetrable wall around the introvert's suffering, making him or her feel momentarily safer—but at the same time, it shuts out potential comfort. The distressed introvert is intent upon minimizing further vulnerability at all costs, and that usually means scrunching away from other people's attention.

As Marti Laney describes in her book *The Introvert Advantage,* introverts have an amazing ability to look like things don't bother them. Introverts are deep feelers and strong reactors, but their protective emotional withdrawal often makes them look calmer and more unruffled than they really feel. Many an introvert has been misunderstood as being unaffected by something because of their reflexive survival mechanism of keeping a straight poker face when most upset.

There is good reason for the introvert's urge to pull back and isolate since introverts gain strength and energy from spending time alone. Contemplation and thinking things through help the introvert pull back together and once again feel centered. If you push an introverted child to interact and explain before finishing this crucial inner work, the introvert will feel pressured and intruded upon, not comforted. Introverts *need* to keep out the other person until they can reorganize enough internally to be able to talk about it.

Unfortunately, other people often feel rejected or confused when the obviously distressed introvert pushes away sympathetic questions or offers of help. These would-be comforters may take the clammed-up introvert's withdrawal personally, making them pull away in frustration. Distance then increases with an erosion of good will between parent and child who deep down need each other very much.

To comfort an introverted kid, one must wait. The role of a patient attendant is a good one to keep in mind. Suffering introverts may find it very hard to interact in the midst of their pain because their inner processing is taking up all their attention. But no matter how brusque the brush-off, one can bet that the introvert is secretly hoping the parent does not give up. Introverts find it difficult to interact when they are hurting, but they do not want to be left alone completely.

To give the introverted child time and room—yet remain available and interested—is like working a NASA shuttle launch. You can't go with them when they leave you behind, but you can always be there to pick them up where they land. And you never ever take your eye off them while they are aloft. The course of an introvert's distress has its own timetable, but your patience and concern give the introvert a profound sense of security. The introverted child needs to know that you noticed, that you did not fall for the stony face or stiff upper lip. Even as they cringe away, they are deeply gratified that someone noticed something was wrong.

Introverts recover through being alone, but they don't like to feel lonely. Later they may tell you what was wrong, but that won't be the most healing part for them. The best part will be the part when you worried about them, knowing what deep currents are flowing beneath those protective walls. To comfort an introverted child, don't push. But don't go away either. Your concern is their runway back into the world.

46 Ungrateful Children

Too much gratitude fastens the mind on the past instead of on the future to be built.

Children don't mean to be ungrateful. They just don't understand what goes into parenting. From their perspective, all the good in their lives seems to flow to them naturally, not through anything special the grown-ups are doing. Children may see their parents working long hours or worrying about money, but they do not really put it together in any kind of meaningful way.

The first seeds of appreciation for one's parents often are sown in a person's twenties, around the time of a first major job or first child. At that point, the newness of adulthood is a challenge, but there is an energizing sense of pride at holding an adult role at long last. In their twenties, children are glad to be out of their parents' hair and at their own helm. They are also pretty sure that they don't need input from Mom and Dad in their careers, relationships, and child-rearing. The future promises them a life of their own creation.

By their thirties, although those same kids still have the confidence of newly hatched adults, they begin to get a feel for the repetitiousness of it all. They now see the value of longer-term goals, and while they defend their independence, they now are willing to see their parents as useful sources of information about important things like buying a house, getting loans, or handling a problem at work. These thirtysomethings value their parents for their knowledge and experience, but they still want to be free to learn on their own.

It isn't until somewhere in the front end of the forties that these children begin to see what it is like to have one's options and freedoms narrowed down by finances and the first hints of real aging. Meanwhile, they realize that alongside these sobering facts, their responsibilities hold constant or actually increase. They might realize what it's like to feel trapped in a job or to give up a dream so that a child can realize his or hers instead. Moments of reflection begin at this age. For the first time in their lives, these adult children understand how hard it can be to be a grown-up day in and day out. They now have an idea how much their parents really gave to them and how much they were loved. Appreciation begins to put down roots as life experience now gives them a taste of just how much responsibility their parents took on.

It is really only in the fifties, when aging and a conservation of energies makes us more contemplative, that middle-aged offspring really begin to get it. They truly see what it feels like to have to keep working way past the point where you want to. They realize now how little control they really had over so many big issues in life and how necessary it is to keep going even when you don't feel like it. They finally feel, at this late age, unmistakable pangs of gratitude for what their parents gave them in their earlier years. Now they know what it cost.

By the sixties and seventies, those same ungrateful children have become their parents' soul siblings in their mutual understanding of the inevitability of human decline. The little narcissisms of earlier life have been sorted through for the most part, and elderly parents and aging children increasingly resemble people who have served in the same war, with much more in common than they could ever have imagined in earlier life. The future meets the past.

The moral of this is: If you treat your children with love and fairness (for the most part) and if your heart is in the right place, it will be a mere forty years or so before they will gladly give you your due. That's when they will truly be able to be grateful and proud of all you did. But up until that point, they are simply too intent on creating their own lives.

Don't be discouraged. They *need* that first forty years of necessary arrogance to do all they will do without looking back. Too much gratitude fastens the mind on the past instead of on the future to be built. Until they are old enough to know better, take comfort from the fact that their gratitude is germinating in a long, slow process that will be all the more beautiful when it finally blooms. They then will know what you never in a million years could tell them in words: how much you loved them and how much you gave. Only when they have loved and given in kind will they arrive at true gratitude, realizing for the first time all they received.

47   Here Come the Zoomers

What do you do with a child who is unimpressed by adult authority?

There's a new kind of kid in town. These quick children would rather self-express than please a grown-up, opposite to how your EI parent conditioned you to behave. They make up their own minds. They are guiltless about their pleasures and cool toward conventional achievement. No wonder their parents are snapping up the parenting books. Conventional parenting is being tested with a new breed of kid: Get ready for the zoomers!

To achievement-oriented parents, it is flabbergasting that carrot-and-stick discipline techniques—the best that behaviorism has to offer—do little but make these kids more entrenched in the behaviors that were causing the problems in the first place. When a parent tries to motivate a zoomer by preaching what is good or desirable, the zoomer is likely to look at them as if to say, "*I'll* be the judge of that." What do you do with a child who is unimpressed by adult authority, takes punishment without internalizing shame, and does not give up his or her point of view in spite of the adult's best coercive efforts? Oh, and by the way, these children *will* happily accept rewards but without the nagging feeling that they owe anything in return. They are a disciplinarian's nightmare.

Contrary to parents' worst fears, these energetic, opinionated children are not antisocial, unattached, or congenitally defiant. They simply are *themselves*. They know what they like and whom they respect (or not), and their primary drive is to meet the needs of their inner self's promptings—as quickly as possible. These children zoom deeply into their passions, and they seem to believe that if something is not self-actualizing, it is not worth doing. They are invariably fast-paced in their areas of special interest but seemingly incapable of motivation or even movement if a task has no personal meaning to them.

Since fear is not the zoomer's primary motivator, it is hard to scare them into conformity. Instead of looking to adults to tell them what is important, the zoomer generation looks *within*. (Is it stimulating? Is it enlivening? Is it *fun?*) What's with these kids? And how come they get to ask if it is *fun* while we adults accept without question the idea that we must *work* our way up the ladder? The answer lies in Abraham Maslow's classic pyramid of human motivation, the hierarchy of needs.

According to Maslow, the needs of human beings are built upon one another like a pyramid, from basic survival needs up through the needs for belonging and love, and finally rise to the apex of the pyramid, the need for self-actualization. Maslow dubbed all the needs below self-actualization as *deficiency motivations*, meaning that people dominated by these needs see life as a struggle to survive, belong, and gain status. Anyone who lives according to deficiency motivations is a perfect candidate for behavioral techniques, such as praise or punishment, because they look *outside* themselves for security and rewards.

Not so the zoomers. They arrived at a time in society when their hard-working parents managed to meet all these children's lower, deficiency-based needs before they were even born. Zoomers *start* life at the top of Maslow's pyramid of needs. This is why approval and honors do not particularly motivate zoomers. Their devoted parents provide a safe home and have already met their esteem needs by viewing them positively no matter what. Zoomers are not pre-occupied with pleasing others in order to belong because their parents have done such a good job making sure these children feel secure in their parents' hearts.

From the time of their first breath, zoomers arrive ready for the next step, the self-actualization that their achievement-oriented, deficiency-motivated parents have not quite made it to (at least not without a fair amount of guilt). You cannot scare zoomers into learning skills in order to earn a living or guilt them into putting others first. Zoomers are not afraid, and they are not guilty. They just do not see life that way. When you think about it, their reality sense is impeccable. We parents have already taken care of their deficiency motivations. From their perspective, why should they need conventional achievement when their parents have made it so clear they already are safe, loved, special, and wonderful? There is no meaningful place for them to go but up to the next step: self-actualization and inner-directedness.

But of course parents worry about what would happen if these zoomer kids suddenly had to make a living. What if there were a disaster, and they had to survive? Would they be able to do it?

Yes, of course they would, because then the zoomer would be responding to a *real* need—with its own driving urgency—that they would feel from within. When survival and security are threatened, self-actualization automatically takes a back seat until safety is restored. Parents can take comfort in the fact that the laws of Maslow's pyramid work in reverse as well. According to need, we can go down as well as up the pyramid.

Zoomer children have transcended what we parents understand as life's system of rewards and punishments. It is not that they are selfish or entitled. They are simply being what it is necessary for them to be, given what already has been prepared for them by their parents. From their perspective, why should they be motivated to accomplish what has already been done? We really cannot expect them to be excited about assembling old puzzles we have already solved for them.

So where does a parent go with this? First, parents should pat themselves on the back for having given their child a leg up to the top of the pyramid. It is a huge generational accomplishment for which any parent can be justifiably proud. Secondly, since many of us in the current adult generation don't get to spend much time in self-actualization, we need to admit that we actually have little idea how to do life at this level. Maybe the zoomers will teach us what it is like up there. If we pay close attention, who knows what new things we may learn about education, parenting, and what really matters in life? Even as we check their homework and make them take out the trash, let's look to the zoomers to show us what it is like to live life from the top.

48 Accept Your Teen's Immaturity

You just want your children to succeed so you can finally relax.

These days, I see many more stressed-out parents worrying about their child's future earlier and earlier. These parents are biting their nails over a low grade or two in middle school and launching into lectures about GPAs and job success at the drop of a hat. By the time high school comes around, these parents agonize over class choices, AP sign-ups, and whether to use college savings to pay for that SAT prep course.

It's a far cry from the old days of less involved parents and unsupervised kids. Back then, teens had a chance to squirm around as they pleased inside the chrysalis of adolescence, having fun with friends, playing games, hanging out, and generally wasting their time. Except it was not a waste of time, at least not developmentally speaking. The primary psychological task of the teen years is to find out who you are apart from Mom and Dad and what kind of life you will be happy with as a freshly minted adult. But overly concerned parents can hardly resist the temptation to reach inside that developmental cocoon and speed things up a bit or at least reposition a limb or two for optimal development.

Do you live in fear that your child will be left behind in the dust of the stampede for limited opportunities for success, whether that be college or jobs? Do you vividly imagine your precious daughter wasting her potential in the backwater of an off-brand college just because she didn't take that chemistry class seriously? Do you envision your angry, lazy, egocentric fourteen-year-old son acting that way with his future boss as you worry yourself sick over normal adolescent behavior? If so, you are part of the rise of the *strategic parent.*

In times past, parents lived in a world where good jobs and companies were available for lifelong careers. College was seen as accessible if you could afford it. But today, we see the competition of a global economy, the inability to afford a little starter apartment with a minimum wage job, and the virtual disappearance of job security. Self-help and parenting books inflame your parental anxieties by suggesting you can mold your children into whatever you want. You might read between the lines that it is up to you to make sure your kids don't fail. You just want your children to succeed so you can finally relax.

Nowadays, strategic parents believe that the stakes are too high for a kid to indulge in an ordinary adolescence. There isn't time for that. The clock is ticking, and the starting gate is filling. Much of ordinary adolescent behavior has come to be seen as a threat to future success.

Yet normal adolescent behavior by definition reflects that a teen is still immature and not good at self-control or future-planning. In an adult, such characteristics would spell trouble, but they are perfectly normal for a fifteen-year-old. Few behaviors in adolescence actually forecast future success or failure. Strategic parents have lost sight of an essential fact: your teen is not grown yet. Wanting to see signs—any signs—of adulthood as early as possible, as a strategic parent, you reinforce starchy conformity and achievement while feeling impatient with normal, shortsighted adolescent behavior.

But thoughtless adolescent behavior is the way many kids find themselves. Strategic parents want to take over a kid's adventure, saying in effect, "You don't have to experience this or try that; just ask me, and I'll tell you what will happen." As strategic parents, we know mistakes can be costly, so we want to help our kids bypass them. In other words, experimentation is no longer worth the risk, not when so much is at stake. Yet all this plotting and planning will not make a dent in the adolescent urge to flap around and knock into things (otherwise known as "learning from experience").

Here's a thought. Maybe we could give our kids some time and have faith in their maturational process. Maybe we could try not to make them feel like failures for being only half grown. Besides, there is no amount of lecturing that will speed up basic brain development. The growing-up process is a messy, back-and-forth affair. Sometimes the only sensible strategy is to sit back and wait for the rest of their immaturity to catch up.

49   Why Einstein Didn't Play Soccer

The child knew that whatever she was going to become in her life would not involve chasing a ball around.

Did you ever see a picture of Einstein, ruddy cheeks glowing, clutching a soccer ball to his chest after kicking the winning goal? I didn't think so. It is not exactly the image we associate with his greatness, is it? We are much more familiar with the picture of him in his study, wild-haired and brilliant in his unapologetic intellectualism. A snapshot of him doing what he did best: thinking.

Einstein was an introvert, a person who derives energy and pleasure from the internal world of his own thoughts. Introversion has nothing to do with being shy or a wallflower; it is the inclination to go within when you need to replenish your energies. Extroverts make a beeline for the external world of people and activities in order to get recharged, but in heavy doses, this same level of activity can be exhausting to the introvert.

Introverts need to turn within and have periods of solitude in which they can process and think about the myriad impressions that have crossed their path that day. Often, introverts truly do not know what they think about a situation right off the bat. They have to retreat a little and figure out what it all means to them. Then they can come back and be quite forceful and articulate about their beliefs. Extroverts, on the other hand, think out loud and arrive at conclusions instantly, subject to correction later if need be.

Needless to say, extroverts do extremely well in group situations. Committee discussions were made for the extroverted style of thinking and interacting. So were soccer matches, community activities, clubs, and PTAs. By some reckoning, extroverts outnumber introverts two to one in our culture. Consequently, definitions of mental health, success, happiness, and good relationships are heavily biased toward extroverted ideals.

Recently, several books and studies have come out looking at the factors that predict happiness and health. Across the board, these factors are an extrovert's dream: lots of social contacts, community involvement, and activities. Does this mean that the introverts, who dread crowds, phone calls, and volunteer work, are destined to be maladjusted? Or sickly? Maybe—just maybe—there's a bit of researcher bias in the kind of factors studied in these studies. Do I detect a not-so-subtle prejudice against introverts' need to spend quiet time alone in order to recharge their batteries and to make their contributions in less people-intensive ways? Maybe the introverted idea of what is meaningful activity differs a bit from the adult equivalent of running around a soccer field.

A woman I know has an extremely bright daughter. For the child's own good, she was signed up for soccer. I guess she was supposed to learn about teamwork, physical fitness, and achieving group goals. But like Einstein, she had other fish to fry. She could be seen sitting under a tree during lulls in practice, reading her books in the little time she had available before having to go kick the ball with the extroverts. This bright girl knew, like Einstein, that whatever she was going to become in her life would not involve chasing a ball around. I think she also knew that her talents and interests might not lie in group goals or even much teamwork.

We are scared that we will not prepare our children for life unless we enroll them in extrovert-sanctioned activities, such as group sports. If they like sports, that's great. But if not, that's great too. Surely there is value in introverted activities as well such as reading, creating, or spending time with one best friend. As far as I can see, soccer teaches people how to behave on a soccer field, not in a boardroom or other bastions of adult power, where entirely different interpersonal skills are needed.

So if you or your little loved one does not crave group activities with lots of running, shouting, and bumping into each other, don't worry. You have other places to spend your energies. Did you know that the average brain when active uses up to 20 percent of the body's glucose stores? Imagine what it is for the above-average thinker. No wonder Einstein didn't play soccer.

Introverts spend their energy inside their heads. They often do not have much left over for social activity, and they need plenty of time alone to recharge their energies if they've had to interact with other people too long. Imagine how drained and frazzled they would feel if they forced themselves to do all the social activities the research says is good for them!

If you or your child is an introvert, find your sustenance where it works best for you. I confess, I don't really know if Einstein played soccer or not, but I do know that he had a few things of his own to contribute. Introverts matter too, so find your own contributions and let the extroverts have the soccer field. You can both be happy and healthy in your own way.

50 Evolution in Our Children

"Normal" means where the parents think evolution should have stopped.

When I listen to parents despairing over their child's fascination with video games and social media, I like to imagine a mother's concern in caveman times about her oddly hairless offspring, worried about how he will ever keep warm. I think about the hominid father wondering how his son will make it through the treetops with those prehensile thumbs of his. I wonder if a Neanderthal mother felt alarmed when her Cro-Magnon daughter's high bulbous forehead set her apart from the other infants.

Apologies for probably having my anthropology all wrong, but parents' universal reaction when evolution shows up in their kid is to want to turn back the clock. Parents only feel secure when their kids seem normal. And normal means where the parents think evolution should have stopped.

Parents know that times have changed and that activities are different, but they still want their children to be the kind of kids the grandparents would approve of. The trouble is that technology has changed things so much in the last two generations that a child's literal physical environment is vastly different. Advertising surrounds us on every usable surface, telling us all to want more and go faster. Nobody is telling people to sit down, pay attention, and comply with authority. It just doesn't sell.

I see no signs of things going backward, with children settling down with a good book and happily doing repetitive homework. I don't see them going back to the landline phone to talk to their friends or giving up TV and video games to play in the yard. Parents who expect their children to enjoy working hard at paper-based tasks are surely courting disappointment.

Why is this? Why is our electronic media body-slamming our beloved paper-based society? Because the human brain has always loved speed and hates to wait. When the technology was slow and the distances were great, people had to wait, to pace themselves, to plan. Slow and careful necessity came to be seen as a virtue.

But the pace of human evolution tends toward speed. The human brain has always lit up in response to anything that broadens its horizons and lets it go really fast. Nothing is going to stand in the way of that. Once we go fast, we are not content with slow. Touch screens trump paper every time.

If we feel worried when our child resists the old work ethic of step-by-step learning, it just means that we have accelerated into the brave new world without realizing it. It does not mean we are bad parents. Education simply has not caught up with the amazing, lightning-fast circuitry that now sparkles in our children's brainpans.

Let's face it. The signs of the world to come suggest that the ability to do ponderous repetition over long periods of time is losing its market value. Whether or not that's a bad thing—evolution will let us know—it is still happening. Patience and planning will always have a role in success, but it may play a smaller part. People who can think that way will probably go the way of engineers and math majors, absolutely essential to the betterment of humanity, but there may not be as many of them.

What may emerge as the preeminent survival skill might be the ability to mentally turn on a dime and to quickly work deals with other people that satisfy both parties. Because there are so many people and companies in the world now, the rigid person who cannot negotiate or spot an opportunity will fall in the dust like the dinosaur they have become. Training our children always to be compliant might have been adaptive in a world where large businesses offered stability and security. Now it is a recipe for obsolescence. We might as well give them a buggy whip as we send them out into the world.

If we feel like we are often haggling or negotiating with our child, maybe it is because that is exactly what evolution is pushing us toward. In the future, our kids may need those skills more than unquestioning obedience. When we see our kids absorbed in video games, reacting instantly to one surprise attack after another, think of them as preparing themselves for a global world of instant change at electronic speed.

In other words, what we call attention deficit disorder (ADD) may be where we've been heading all along. Knowing how to enjoy and pursue quick and superficial social contacts (like Facebook and Twitter) may turn out to be the best way to prosper in this global environment. Certainly, the traders and explorers in the old days were among the fittest for survival, as it turned out, working the outermost edge of social evolution with great benefit for us all.

It remains to be seen if this will continue to be the direction of our evolution, but barring a technological catastrophe of some sort, can you really see it slowing down or kids becoming more docile and respectful of authority? In prehistoric times, the evolving brains that craved novelty and speed kept our species competitive for survival. It worked so well that humans ultimately were able to create their own environments, not just adapt to what was there.

The lifestyle the young human brain likes is fast, stimulating, and worldwide. Our children have smelled the change in the air and are responding like all new generations have responded: eagerly flourishing in the new environment. They may be adapting to their environment faster than we can keep up. But isn't that what parents should want for their children? As far as evolution is concerned, a child's primary job is not to please the grandparents but to be ready for the future.

51 Graduation for Parents

You may think your worry is about them, but maybe it is about you.

You may think that high school graduation is all about the kids, but they are not the only ones leaving the nest this spring. Parents are graduating too, ready or not, especially if your child will be leaving home for college or a new job. Graduations are the end of a life phase at any age, and there is an art to doing them well.

Children cost time, money, and energy, but they give you an all-important mission in life. While one study found that childless couples reported higher life satisfaction, people with children reported having more meaning in their lives. Instead of the quick pleasure of doing what you want, you find meaning in contributing to your kids' future welfare.

Life with dependent children is vastly simplified. Decisions are made on the basis of how things might affect the kids. Limiting your choices is one of the things children do best. Restrictions on your freedom give an odd kind of security, like having a map with clearly marked routes instead of a vast unexplored territory. There are a few things kids absolutely need, and these things often edge out what you might prefer to do on your own. After a while, you get used to following the map of their needs.

Then they grow up and leave, taking your map with them.

It is a little like getting released from a job you thought you would have for the rest of your life. What that feels like will depend on how identified you were with your parenting role. It might be a relief, like the person in a convertible I saw with the license plate *KIDZRGON*. But it might also feel like "Hello, freedom! Goodbye, meaningfulness."

As children mature, their job is to need you less and less. You are responsible only for the beginning of their lives, not the rest of it. When the adolescent part of a child's life is wrapping up, you begin to mentally graduate from parent to bystander. You are no longer their safety net; you have graduated to being a spotter. Kids may still need financial help or occasional advice and suggestions, but parents at some point must sit on their hands and let it unfold.

The essential question becomes, Do you trust them? Do you trust that somewhere deep inside them is a force for maturity, even if it's not looking like that at the time? Do you trust that ultimately they will learn from their mistakes and figure out life's consequences? Do you trust that they will rise to the level that is just right for them, all things considered?

Many people answer these questions with a "Yes, but…" We hope that our children will be able to survive out there, but their behavior so far may not inspire confidence. Raising a child to the point of graduation is like being in on the sausage-making and then being expected to not think about its origins when it arrives on your breakfast plate. It just does not seem possible that all those years of childish behavior are going to add up to a capable adult.

Yet that is job number one for the graduating parent. Somehow your disbelief must be suspended in the service of your child creating his or her own adult story. As your legal responsibilities to your children end, you begin to worry how they will handle being legally responsible for themselves. If their bedrooms are any indication, you may fear complete chaos. Somehow you have to trust that organization and getting up on time will happen if you let it. You have to trust that there will be things they want as adults that will motivate them into maturity. You may not believe this, but you have to try. Imagining your children's eventual maturity gives them faith in themselves. You can believe in them before they show any signs of deserving it.

Now let's go a little deeper. You might think your concern is about them, but maybe it is about you.

Maybe you are terrified about what you will do when you no longer have the mission of looking out for your child's safety and well-being. Who will you be without that worry? What unexplored parts of yourself and your life may come to the forefront? Are you nervous about a void you do not want to face?

Facing the void is an important part of any life transition, as William Bridges talks about in his excellent book, *Transitions*. When the old way has come to an end and we cannot go back (a nice definition of graduation, by the way), there is a highly uncomfortable period of not knowing what's coming next. We may find that we long for the safety of what we did before. For your children's sake, however, you must keep facing forward into your own void, trusting that, just as your kids find their adult way, you will find your post-parenting way. Until you accept your own graduation to bystander-spotter, you will keep seeing your children as children when they have really become budding adults.

Finding a new way forward and celebrating your parental transition is one of the best graduation gifts you can give your kids. They don't need a new car as much as they need your willingness to go forward without them. As a young adult, knowing that you have a parent who has confidently turned responsibility for your life over to you can be an incredibly freeing experience. It does not mean that parents never help kids nor even that you miraculously stop worrying about them. It just means that their life is no longer your life, and at some deep level, you accept that. Like a gym spotter, you may still have to step in and help prevent a catastrophic event, but then you step back and do your best to resume bystander-mode.

Your message to them needs to be "You'll get it; just keep trying." It is the same message you need to tell yourself when life after parenting seems a little pale and you don't know what you are going to do next. It is a normal feeling after parental graduation. You, like your kids, need time to figure it out.

PART III

Coping with Challenges

Meet Life on Its Own Terms

You welcome the challenges you choose to take on. But the ones that catch you by surprise will strengthen you the most. Many times, overcoming adversity comes down to a small adjustment in your approach, a little tweak to your attitude. Then you find that your happiness, like your success, often lies in your own hands.

52 It's a Wild World

Honor those times when you run out of map and become an explorer by default.

When life is going according to plan, we have a routine, we understand the game, and we are pretty sure how to keep our comforts coming. When we know what to do and what will happen next, it is easy to feel confident. And when we feel confident, it is just a hop, skip, and jump to feeling virtuous. After all, we must be doing the right thing if the goodies keep dropping.

But my heart goes out to the people who show up in my office, confidence shot, feeling bad about themselves because some unexpected twist of events has left them stunned by life. They have that shell-shocked face, that expression that says, *I thought I was doing everything right.* They look existentially surprised, as if to say, *How could this have happened to me?* Usually they have come for help only after exhausting their own attempts to make sense out of the unexpected turn their lives have taken. They search for cause and effect, as if discovering guilt or responsibility will get them back on track again. They are confused by life developments that they did not see coming.

In prosperous countries, it is easy to believe that we can live in a controlled, predictable world for much of our lives. If we are hard workers, we will succeed. If we are good parents, our kids will turn out well. If we follow the rules, life will purr around our ankles in domesticated bliss. It seems so simple and straightforward that it is all too easy to blame ourselves when our expectations are turned upside down. But when we do that, we are forgetting a simple fact: We still live in a wild world.

Just because you are living under a roof does not mean *life* has been tamed. In the old days, wildness took the form of dark forests and things with teeth.

Today, you may worry less about those dangers, but that does not mean that you call the shots.

The early explorers and settlers understood this, forging ahead through mishaps and misjudgments, experimenting and learning as they entered each new territory. They often did not know what to expect, but they did know that unpredictability was going to be part of the challenge. They probably didn't take time to be too self-critical because they would just be glad to be surviving under very trying circumstances.

In your own life, honor those times when you run out of map and become an explorer by default. That's when you can remember that life is still a wild affair, unfazed by your plans and habits. Unexpected things happen all the time, just as they have for eons. Many of them you can prepare for, but some of them you cannot.

The point is that you are not always to blame when things happen that are a part of being alive in a wild world. You are not bad or incompetent when things keep you guessing or catch you by surprise. Not everything that happens to you can be foreseen or prevented, and life is too complicated and spontaneous to stay in your lap for long.

When life gets bigger than what you can control, it is helpful to remember that every settler and explorer was as scared as you are. You may find yourself in places without a map or compass, falling back on instinct alone to guide you. At these times, you can call upon your origins as a wild survivor, accepting the unpredictable and accidental, while you keep moving forward to look for better living. Sometimes you will make mistakes or not see something coming, but that's because you are a part of this world, not the master of this world.

The best survivors and settlers knew that they could plan for some things but not everything. They remind us that the world is just wild enough to set a person back when he or she least expects it. It takes the pressure off to remember that life's wildness and risks impact everyone.

Resilience and confidence do not come from organizing your life so that the unexpected does not occur. These capacities develop from accepting yourself and others as fellow explorers in uncharted territory. When you take a survivor's approach, you appreciate and respect the wildness and unpredictability that intrude at times into everyone's lives. You give room to the wild world and don't take it personally when it reveals itself to you. Remember, as wild as the world can be, your ancestors were wild as well, and it's nice to know you still have what it takes.

53 The Realm of the Required

When life demands a response, it doesn't ask which one you feel comfortable making.

Winston Churchill once said, "Sometimes it is not enough to do your best. Sometimes you must do what is required." He was a man who knew a thing or two about surviving adversity under extraordinary conditions. When you are fighting for survival or other high stakes, it hardly matters what you think you can do or how well you think you can do it. All that matters is what must be done.

All of us have our own ideas about what we believe we can accomplish and how much we think we can stand. Most of us feel like we are capable of only so much exertion, and our assumption is that if we try hard and do our best, we have done all that we can do.

Perhaps it would be more true to say that we have done all that we *think* we can do—or all that we are *comfortable* doing. Or all that could reasonably be *expected* of us. But we probably have not done all that we *can* do.

In life's most difficult situations, you don't get to hold on to your opinion about what you think you can do. Before you know it, you are in over your head, and things are happening so fast you no longer have time to quibble about what is reasonable effort and what is necessary for survival. You just start doing. You have been catapulted from the genteel land of sincere effort into the gritty realm of the required.

Human beings—who have been on this earth a long time, and profitably so—are endowed with a survival overdrive gear that kicks in when we or someone we love is facing a serious threat. Most of us do not even know we have this gear. We think we are a little four-cylinder unit that is only equipped for trips to the store. But human history contradicts this. History says that humankind is the biggest, baddest, all-wheel-drive vehicle going. When life gets rough, human beings shift down and pull whatever power is needed to get traction.

You may believe you don't have exceptional mental or physical strength simply because not much of it is required for ordinary life. But when things get bad enough or your loved ones are at risk, you suddenly have a lot in common with Churchill. You pull it together, and instead of worrying whether your best will be good enough, you just start doing what is required.

But we don't always do that willingly. Sometimes you may have great resistance to taking on the supreme effort of what is needed. Perhaps you hate to give up comforting traditional roles that shield you from realizing how much you are capable of under duress. Maybe you want to turn to authority figures for leadership, expecting them to save the day. But what a shock it is when you realize that *you* are the best one to deal with the crisis.

None of us really likes to go beyond what we think should be asked of us. We instinctively resist anything that is perceived as an unfair burden or the sole responsibility for fixing a problem. Most people have to get over this hump of resentment before they start to function effectively in the realm of the required. Once the resentment calms down, however, you face the simplicity of just doing what needs to be done next.

Sometimes, your supreme effort may involve something dramatic like lifting a car off someone. But other strengths are more often required, such as protracted patience or biting your tongue. These frustrations and deprivations are also feats of endurance that often go beyond what you thought you could tolerate. But for the person who ultimately deals with these situations successfully, tremendous psychological growth and enhanced self-respect is the payoff.

When you find yourself unexpectedly challenged, you can feel resentment and anxiety as you are forced into roles for which you never signed up. Yet it can be exhilarating when it dawns on you that *you* are the one who has what it takes, the one with the most sensible ideas or the emotional stamina to do what needs to be done. Once you do it, you are empowered. You find out just how underchallenged you had been in your previous roles.

You may like to function at the level where doing your best is good enough. But sometimes you are ushered into the realm of the required. When life demands a response, it doesn't ask which one you feel comfortable making. It requires the supreme effort for the situation and nothing less. Sir Winston would tell you that human beings are designed to do exactly that. You will remember your strength as soon as circumstances require you to use it.

54 Cultivate Your Mule Mind

If the workload is more than the mule can do, it won't do it.

My father was a businessman, but he also raised beef cattle on the family farm. His wisdom came from these rural roots, and he enjoyed passing it along to his kids. He once told me about the difference between horses and mules. My father said that, in the old days, the smart farmer would not buy a horse to plow his fields. Instead he would get a good mule if he could.

The benefit of a mule over a horse is the fact that a mule will stop when it gets tired, while a horse will work itself to death. A wise farmer knew that for the momentary inconvenience of a stubborn mule that refused to work further, he got an automatic protection on his investment. No mule is going to work until it expires.

A mule is not a beautiful animal. It is big like a horse but not graceful and donkey-like without being cute. But what a mule does have is an uncompromising respect for its physical limits. In spite of its strength and hardiness, it balks at an overload. It does not care how mad you get or what you think of its character. If it is more than the mule can do, it won't do it.

The horse, on the other hand—noble animal that it is—takes its cue from what its owner wants. If the job is to keep working no matter what, it will. Horses will work or race until they drop just because they can. The horse will ignore its exhaustion in order to keep up with the herd (or owner). By the time a horse realizes it has done too much, it can be too late.

This characteristic of horses may be one reason why little girls on the cusp of puberty fall so deeply in love with these beautiful, bighearted animals. Little girls are probably intuiting something they may share with the sensitive horse when they reach adulthood: grace and power used unstintingly in the service of other people. Perhaps young girls resonate with a being that gives up its wild freedom in order to belong to and care for others.

You don't hear much about girls falling in love with mules, but maybe we ought to push this. Instead of encouraging little girls to focus on flowing manes and tails, we could tell them to use their strengths on their own behalf. Freed from the horse's distraction of being so beautiful, mules have learned to pay attention to their insides. Women can too.

Whether daydreamers or tomboys, little girls are originally filled with their own agendas. Before they are taught to be so self-sacrificing, girls are as naturally full of themselves as anybody else. Like the mules, they have no interest in working long hours for nothing, and they are always looking for ways to enjoy themselves. But when the cultural pressure starts to define their worth by social groups and romance, girls lose their nerve. They start thinking they are going to be left behind in some great race if they don't get other people to love them. Social belonging can begin to matter so much to girls and boys alike that they will disregard how they really feel.

Both girls and boys can turn into people who give up too much. They learn to feel proud of self-sacrifice, trying to be good spouses and devoted parents. They will keep going in the service of others until their big hearts break from the loss of themselves. Like the overworked, loyal horse, they can lose their spark and health yet not understand why they feel so bad. Customs have fooled women especially into believing that if they do a good job of sacrificing for others, they will be happier and more fulfilled. Some men believe it too. This is like telling a horse that the harder and longer he runs, the better he will feel.

Exhaustion and listlessness are nature's way of saying you have given too much. Sickness is often the only guilt-free way people can be excused from running themselves to death. If you become mentally or physically ill, you finally have permission to pay attention to that little voice that told you years ago you should have stopped. Unfortunately, many hope that the people who love them will notice and rein them in before it is too late. They wonder why no one sees they are about to drop. Is no one paying attention to what this race is costing them?

No. Nine times out of ten, no one is paying attention to what the race is costing you. Only you can do that. And that self-checking is just what horses do not do. Sometimes horses must be forcibly prevented from running their hearts out; they prance and pull, asking for more when they should have quit hours ago. They keep being eager and strong even when they are on their last atom of reserves. Think about the social ideal of a good woman, for example: it is the woman who keeps on giving, not the woman who keeps on living. Or consider the fantasy of the good man, who is supposed to provide for others to the point of near collapse.

I prefer the mule's approach. The mule just stops. He might be willing to work more later, but for right now, he could not care less what that field looks like. His animal wisdom says that if he wants to live long, he better pay attention to what his muscles are saying.

Anyone raised by an EI parent needs to learn to do the same thing. It can be harder for women when so much of their energy is spent on *emotional* work. When what you do is not visible or measurable in terms of workload, no one but you can see what things cost emotionally. It is not like having a sore muscle or pulled tendon. Instead, you feel emotionally drained, zapped, exhausted, or whipped. By the time others notice, it may have already shown up in the form of depression, anxiety, or a host of psychosomatic illnesses. But by the time these symptoms arrive, I guarantee it is late in the last quarter of the race, and someone has kept moving your finish line farther and farther out.

You need to learn how to notice emotional fatigue somewhere before the halfway pole. The culture will run you to death if you let it, so you have to learn to say no. Mulishness must be deliberately cultivated if you have a noble horse nature.

To have a healthy mule mind, keep asking yourself, *Is this too much? Am I getting tired? What is making me so tired, and how can I do less of it?* Believe me, you do not have to worry about becoming a lazybones, because family and culture will never stop driving you on. You are the only one who can sit down in the field and refuse to go further. Remember, no farmer is stronger than a mule that has had enough. It won't kill the farmer to accommodate once in a while, but it might kill the mule to do it all the time.

Pay attention to your inner signals of fatigue or depletion and take them seriously. Nine-tenths of life is a field that can wait, not a race to be won.

55   When to Back Off

Take a deep breath and mentally detach from the intoxication of your own adrenaline.

Do you ever wish you had a little angel on your shoulder to tell you to back off before the next thing you do makes the situation worse? When we get angry or focus on our resentments, we speak and act in ways that get other people to feel as negatively as we do in that moment. Later, of course, we may regret what we said or how we said it, but at the time, we are like lemmings going over the cliff; everything in us is rushing toward disaster.

But surely, you may think, *we cannot just sit back and keep our feelings bottled up. Are we supposed to turn the other cheek when the other person is just blatantly* wrong?

Well, let's think about what you really want. Do you want more conflict or less? Do you want to pursue your life goals, or would you rather put your energy into fighting with people? You only have so much energy, and the creative power you use to promote fighting and resentment is power you could devote to getting what you want. Would you rather create your desirable outcome or teach other people a lesson?

In the future, let's say you decide to forgo revenge in favor of desirable outcomes. How will you know when you are starting down the path of conflict again? How will you know when you are beginning to move *away* from finding a peaceful solution?

In the absence of angels on our shoulders, we have to pay attention to our adrenal glands. The adrenals sit in the general area of our mid torso, and they secrete adrenaline for the famous flight-or-fight response. When the adrenals squirt out this transformative hormone (think Incredible Hulk), it gives us a very distinct physical sensation. Our whole system tenses, and a thrill of dread and anger rushes through our midsection. We act like we are facing down a bear, but what really may be happening is that a friend has let us down or a spouse may have said something insensitive when tired.

The adrenals care nothing about the nuances of modern realities; all they sense is a bear. All they care about is making sure you win, with as much force as is necessary to make sure that bear is dead twenty times over. Adrenals only know that if you are in a threatening situation, the thing to do is fight until your survival is completely guaranteed, whatever it takes.

The problem is that adrenals react blindly. They do one thing—fight—very well, but they never think about the future or its consequences. They cannot think because they are little hormone-secreting masses of tissue that function completely in the dark.

When there is really a bear, I must admit, I would trade in my brain for my adrenals in a second. However, approximately 99.9 percent of what you face on a daily basis concerning other people is better solved through thinking than through our adrenals. So the best time to walk away from a situation, figuratively speaking, is as soon as you feel that distinctive adrenaline release in your gut. Nothing interpersonal is going to get solved when you are in that mode, and there is a good chance you are about to make things worse.

Unfortunately, adrenaline is designed to make us feel powerful and confident no matter what. Once it starts its effect on your brain, adrenaline convinces you it knows just what to do to settle this problem once and for all. You don't just feel mighty; you feel *certain* that you know what to do. For better or worse, adrenaline annihilates self-doubt. That sensation of certainty makes you not think twice about what you do next.

But if it is a relationship issue, thinking twice is the preferable strategy. Your goal is not to wipe out the other person, not to render them non-threatening for all time, but to work something out with them so you can still talk to each other at dinner that night. Other people react to forcefulness with resistance and anger, and then all you have is *two* sets of adrenal glands flopping around in a puddle of aggression hormones.

As a rule of thumb, try this: if it's not a bear, disregard your adrenals' urgings. If the problem involves a loved one instead of a large, hairy predator, that visceral adrenal sensation is best used as a signal to halt our attack and back off. Tell your loved one you need a moment to think, and then go think. Ask yourself how you want this to turn out. If you want a solution instead of hard feelings, first check your adrenal sensations. If you find them squirting away, resist the impulse to blurt and refocus your thoughts on the positive outcome you would like from the situation.

With practice, you will be able to take a deep breath and mentally detach from the intoxication of your own adrenaline. Remember to try and think about what you really want (a peaceful solution), not what your adrenals want (war). The time to back off is as soon as your adrenals kick in.

56 Appreciate Your Threshold Guardians

As soon as you attempt something worthwhile, a threshold guardian will appear.

New adventures follow a pattern, and all our best stories come from it. Examine your favorite movie or book, and you will find the pattern, even though you were not aware of it when focused on enjoyment. The pattern is known as the *hero's journey*, perhaps best described in Joseph Campbell's classic book *The Hero with a Thousand Faces*. The hero—the main character in the story—gets the calling to seek something precious. For Ulysses in *The Odyssey*, he wanted to get back home after the war; for Jason, it was the Golden Fleece; for you, it might be the new job, living on your own, taking that class, or recovering from illness. Even aging is a classic hero's journey as we inch forward into unfamiliar territory.

But there is a catch. Before heroes even set sail to realize their dream quest, they will run into the *threshold guardians*. The sole purpose of a threshold guardian is to test your mettle, to see if you are ready for your own hero's journey. As soon as you attempt something worthwhile, a threshold guardian will appear in one form or another. It is not enough to be willing to meet the challenge; you must also convince the threshold guardian that you have what it takes.

Many people get discouraged and lose their nerve when their dream takes more work than they thought it would. You can see it in their eyes when they first realize that the path is not as easy as it looked. Their face says it all: *it shouldn't have to be this hard.* But wait! Yes, it does! That's the whole point! No self-respecting threshold guardian is going to let you just waltz into a new life without pushing you around a little. Ulysses had to outwit the Cyclops and other threats before he could return home. You may just have to battle unreturned phone calls, negative comments, and insufficient funds. But the lesson for the hero's journey is the same for us: if you give up when the threshold guardians appear, you'll never win the prize.

The hero's quest teaches us that the ultimate prize is not the only important purpose; an equally important goal is the strengthening that occurs as we take on each threshold guardian. As you stand up to your threshold guardians, you face things about yourself—not all of them complimentary. Encountering a threshold guardian is a sobering experience. You find out just how scared and weak you really feel along with all the infantile expectations that keep you feeling like a victim. You will be tempted to step aside and go back to envying others who got what they wanted.

The good news is that *everyone* encounters threshold guardians. Nobody is exempt, regardless of appearances. Threshold guardians arrive in many forms. They might be a broken-down car on the way to the interview, but they can also come in the form of bad relationships or low self-esteem. In one way or another, they try to convince you that you do not have what it takes, that you should just give up and go back home. Negative self-talk is a perfect example of a threshold guardian, a voice that tells you why you weren't cut out to be a success story.

The best-kept secret is that threshold guardians are really on your side. They will not let you go forward without first developing some courage and determination. Like the drill sergeant or the tough professor, the threshold guardians subject you to a dry-run survival challenge before you have to make it in the real world. If they made it too easy, you might get flattened on your first day out. Without their toughening treatment, you might not be able to overcome discouragement later on.

If you find yourself feeling hopeless or like giving up, you have just met a threshold guardian. Call it by name. Let it know you understand what it's trying to do. Then ask it to step aside and go after that fuller life for yourself. It *is* supposed to be this hard. It is the only way that dreamers turn into heroes.

57 Football Lessons

There's happiness in meaningful struggles, even when the going gets rough.

I confess that my interest in football is directly proportional to what is at stake. For me, the playoffs and Super Bowl are exciting, as is a Hail Mary pass or a touchdown against all odds. But why are die-hard fans passionate about even mediocre games?

I asked a football fan what he found entertaining about the time-consuming struggle for a few yards at a time. All that positioning back and forth? All that inching toward an elusive line? It was like watching paint dry. What kept him and other fans so transfixed for months on end? He said it was the process. He explained that watching the process was as fascinating and important to him as how many points were scored. That slow gain of territory was the drama of watching highly motivated people fight for the right to go where they wanted to go—their opponents' end zone. *Ah,* I thought, *there's a deeper truth that football has to teach us.*

It is uniquely human to enjoy challenging pursuits that involve long periods of process with no immediate payoff. There are many activities—writing, art, raising children, fitness, and business, to name a few—where it matters greatly what you do on the front end long before you reach the final payoff or finished product. It's crucial to keep trying, even if your progress is glacially slow. There's happiness in meaningful struggles, even when the going gets rough.

The slow, brutal work of football is meaningful because it is about attaining a difficult goal by giving it your all. The game abounds in persistence, strategy, tactics, and resilience. Football is all about bouncing back. Football players can also show you how to look confident when you are not, and they never give up prematurely, regardless of the writing on the wall. The ritual of positioning for the last down with seconds on the clock demonstrates how to keep your intent, even in the face of defeat. This kind of resolve keeps your purpose clear and your morale up, whether inside or outside a stadium.

Football shows you how to keep going when you're getting roughed up by other people who want their goals as much as you do. It tells you that your desires are just as important as anyone else's and therefore worth fighting for. Like all sports, football affirms that you are entitled to go after what you want. More importantly, football reminds you not to become a victim when you start losing or if other people are mean to you.

Football shows you that winning is hard because lots of other people are also trying to win. You must be willing to fight for your own yardage because other people are not always going to step in to help you. And whenever you feel like you're failing, football is clear about what to do next: set up your next play and keep pursuing your goal.

Football also teaches you to develop different aspects of yourself. Sometimes in life, you are like the star quarterback throwing an eighty-yard pass in the last minutes of the game or the running back in full stride catching a ball looking backward. But you also need to train parts of yourself to be like burly linebackers, halting the momentum of opponents or adverse circumstances. As a player in the game of life, you may experience shame when you drop, fumble, or miss a pass, but the game will go on regardless. Nobody does it perfectly all the time. Remember that in sports, you're killing it when you are doing well *most* of the time.

If you want to enjoy football more, watch for these lessons in how to conduct yourself when it feels like life is blocking your progress. Watch and appreciate the boring but necessary positioning, the strategies that don't pay off, and the determination to keep pushing forward. More than that, let the best players show you how to manage yourself when life tackles you, even if a flag is thrown. What's the biggest lesson? When you only get four chances to go ten yards, make them count.

58 Life's Tuition

Your mistakes are a little easier to bear if you look at your regrets as down payments on wisdom.

A friend was telling a group of us about how she freed herself from an undesirable real estate deal by forfeiting her deposit and walking away. While she supposed she should feel horrible about her loss of money, she actually found herself giggling with relief over her narrow escape from what would have been a regretted decision. Another person in the group commented about the financial loss, "It was your tuition." The lost money was our friend's fee for the lesson learned: Get out of bad decisions as fast as possible.

This remark was profound in its implication. What if we looked at life this way? What if, instead of seeing ourselves as losing money, we saw ourselves as paying for experience? What if the point of life was not never to make a bad decision but to learn how to handle it afterward? . .

Of course, our life tuition is not just about money. It could be anything that we invest, down payments such as our attention, time, or energy. We are accustomed to thinking that the only good outcome is a profitable return on our investment, but that is not the whole story. A few hasty, costly bad decisions early in life can be just the ticket to more mature caution later on. There is only one way to know how it feels when you make a rash decision: You pay for it.

We accept as a matter of course that education costs money. There is little valuable learning that comes free of charge. Ask anyone who has gotten any kind of reputable degree or training certification. If you want to go to a trade school, a private school, or a technical school, you pay for it. If you want to go to college or graduate school, you have to pay for it. We hardly expect that kind of knowledge to be given to us free of charge. But when it comes to learning how to be effective in the world, we somehow think we should know it all before we begin. We come down pretty hard on ourselves when we make a mistake. But your mistakes can be a little easier to bear if you look at your regrets as down payments on wisdom.

Of course, just as in college, going to class does not always mean you are getting the degree. Making mistakes does not mean a person is learning. Some people pay life's tuition heedlessly, taking nothing but electives, and never wonder why the same old problems keep happening over and over. They meet their failures with a shrug instead of a pang. Their lack of curiosity and minimal self-awareness ensure they will have one year's experience twenty times instead of twenty years of experience.

The trick is to feel bad enough about a mistake to not want to repeat it but not so bad that you feel hopeless about yourself. When things do not go as you'd hoped, it is a good idea to stop for a moment and ask yourself what you have learned and what you paid to learn it. If you learn from painful experiences, they create opportunities for more competent living.

In many cases, the experiences you regret the most, the ones full of sorrow or embarrassment, are also the ones that bring you closer to new realizations about yourself and others. This kind of knowledge hits you with a special force, as what is truly real snaps back into focus, dispelling illusion and distortion. As painful as it is, that kind of realization is always worth the price of admission. The tuition is steep, but so is the radical self-growth that occurs when you start perceiving things accurately. People pay tuition in psychotherapy hoping for exactly this kind of experience, trying to figure out why they are making repeated mistakes in the business of living and how to find a more effective method.

So the next time you make a real doozy of a bad decision, especially one that costs you money, consider it an educational expense. You may feel like you are qualifying for a doctorate in dumb mistakes, but don't let that stop you from earning your credits. Quiz yourself after things go wrong and get a good grade in learning from it. Then the tuition is a bargain.

Lower Your Stress

You can approach life in a way that takes the edge off and helps you find a more natural rhythm. Adopting a self-compassionate outlook is one of the best ways to feel less stress. Instead of judging and finding fault with yourself, you can lower your stress by using a gentler approach with yourself.

59 The Stressaholic

You feel guilty and lazy for not doing something constructive every single second.

All addicts will tell you that their drug of choice made them feel good before it started taking their life away. That's easy to understand when it's something like alcohol or cocaine, but the same is true of stress addiction. Stress is usually seen as a negative, so you may wonder how it could ever be experienced as something desirable, something you could get hooked on. Of course, not everyone becomes addicted to stress, just as not everyone's life is changed by their first taste of alcohol. But for those who are susceptible, the rush of stress hormones can be positively intoxicating.

Stress stimulates us and creates heightened sensory attention along with speeded up cognitions. Our many responsibilities can make us feel important: our sense of urgency gives our life a certain meaningfulness as we push ourselves to get everything done. We feel like we're playing for high stakes, with a smidgen of grandiosity, as if no one else could possibly do what needs to be done as well as we can. If we try to slow down or not stress ourselves so much, we begin to feel a little down and empty, a depressive malaise that is actually addiction withdrawal.

You may not realize you are addicted to stress or any other intoxicant because the longer you do it, the more adjusted you become to it. It seems that it is hardly affecting you at all. For instance, I have heard it said that some people don't have a drinking problem because they can drink all night and not show it. The problem is that people who really hold their liquor can do that because they have been drinking a lot for a long time and their physiology has adapted to it. The same goes for stressed-out people who pride themselves on staying super busy and constantly productive. This high level of activity and sense of nonstop commitment starts to feel like the norm rather than a warning sign.

The problem with addictions is that physical tolerance for the substance goes up and up, while damaging and lethal thresholds stay the same. This means that there is an upper limit or ceiling on the amount of intoxicant our bodies can physically stand, *whether one is feeling its effects or not*. So people who are not noticing the effects of their addiction could still be approaching the lethal zone.

The same is true with stress. A little bit of stress feels challenging and invigorating, often increasing meaningfulness, purpose, and a sense of importance. But as responsibilities increase as you go through life, you start to habituate to higher and higher levels of stress. Staying busy and feeling pressured begin to feel like the right way to live, as though anything less might make you feel vaguely worthless. But just like with drugs or alcohol, there is an upper limit on your tolerance for stress, no matter how used to it you become. Stress-related symptoms such as anxiety, sleeplessness, nervous overeating, worry, and impaired concentration begin to occur in the first stages of overdosing on stress. Later on, physical limits are reached, and body systems start to suffer. Yet all the while, *stressaholics* may not see the connection between lifestyle and these symptoms. The high level of stress just feels normal.

If you are a stressaholic, you have an exaggerated sense of pressure and self-criticism, which you seek to relieve through the distraction of your addiction. You probably have a mean-spirited inner voice that is exceptionally judgmental and demanding and that says that your worth is something yet to be proven, not something inherent in just being alive. Alcoholics drink to make the voice shut up, while stressaholics work and worry themselves to death to keep one jump ahead of this inner judge. As a stressaholic, you may feel worthwhile only when you are virtuously busy, secretly hoping that other people will be impressed by your demanding schedule.

The real payoff of any addiction, whether a substance or a superhuman level of responsibility, is that it anesthetizes you to your deep doubts about your own worth and lovability. Love feels very conditional to any addict, and stressaholics use very busy and overcommitted lives as a subconscious way of finally being good enough. But ultimately, your addiction leads to profound self-neglect as you keep trying to earn other people's regard.

Stressaholics often find it difficult to slow down to more reasonable levels of responsibility and activity. You feel guilty and lazy for not doing something productive every single second. Yet when you finally try to pay more attention to your feelings and needs, you may be amazed at how numb you have become. You finally realize that you have been able to manage an insane workload only by ignoring the warning signals of emotional and physical distress. If you can reconnect with this inner communication, you start noticing the pain of stress and can ease up before any lasting damage is done.

It is worth the effort to wean yourself off excessive stress because, just like with any other addiction, stressaholism will make you ignore the emotional needs of other people just as you ignore your own. Having a connected emotional life with other people means slowing down enough to enjoy experiences with them, not just performing activities around them. Recovering from the stress habit means rescuing your life and self-worth from impossible standards and learning to love and support yourself just for being here. You also will be kinder to other people as a result, a surefire sign of recovery in any addiction.

60 Ninety Seconds to Feel Better

Why do emotional upsets last so long?

We are all experts in fight-or-flight, and our brains are hair-triggered to set off these reactions. Once we feel a jolt of fear or a surge of anger, it can be hard to calm down. In fact, these are two of the hardest emotions to shake once they take hold. But according to brain scientist Jill Bolte Taylor in her fascinating book *My Stroke of Insight,* these gripping emotions are triggered, run their course, and are cleared from the body in about ninety seconds.

Most of us, however, do not experience anxiety or anger in minute-and-a-half bursts. Instead, our anxiety can last all night, and our anger can keep going for days. But if an intense emotion can flood the body and be flushed out again in under two minutes, why do our emotional upsets last so long?

The reason is that when we are angry, we look for more reasons to keep being angry. It is the same with fear. If we feel afraid, we keep looking at the outside world through the eyes of fear. By fixating on our distress, we can keep our painful feelings going way past their expiration date. This is how we maintain an angry mood and magnify our fears past all reason.

Because emotion is an intense neurochemical activity inside our very own body, our instinct is to take it completely seriously. A few squirts of neurotransmitter in our brain, and our view of the world is drenched in the emotional color of the moment. We usually do not wonder if our emotions are giving us the straight scoop. If we feel it, it must be so. We accept knee-jerk feeling reactions at face value and then look for justification to keep feeling upset.

Even when our mental and physical health suffers from our distress, we usually don't perceive that we have any choice in the matter. We continue to believe that our emotions are telling us how it really is. If that means we live with our stomachs in knots or our heads aching with pain, so be it. We amplify our feelings by telling ourselves an upsetting story about our emotional reactions. As we tell the story to ourselves about why we feel the way we do, we become even more deeply involved in it, much like watching an engrossing movie. Now our original emotion is supported by a cast of thousands. We are as proprietary about our personal emotional story as the best screenwriters.

It's not so important whether you react to something but what you do next with that reaction. Your physiology may not give you much of a choice about how you feel in the first ninety seconds, but it is definitely up to you how you feel after that. You can do all sorts of things to feel better, such as examining the validity of your feelings, seeking advice and emotional support, looking for solutions, or simply calming yourself down. You just can't do all that in less than ninety seconds.

In the heat of the moment, ninety seconds seems like an eternity. Think about the last time you were really upset. Now imagine sitting with that feeling and counting to ninety. Slowly. During those ninety moments, you probably wouldn't have much faith that you would be feeling better anytime soon. That's why it is good to have the knowledge that you will calm down if only you don't prolong it.

Many people worry that giving up their intense emotional reactions will make them less lively and vital. They think that if they start to manage their emotions, they will become deadly dull. They think being upset signals full living, but what it's really signaling is stress. These people are mistaking feeling adrenaline for feeling alive.

The next time you find yourself getting very upset, try to remember the ninety-second rule. You may have to tolerate ninety seconds of adrenaline, but after that, you can feel better if you choose to. The best shortcut to that calm is to remember that strong opinions about what just happened are not helpful. Even though it may not feel like it during the first ninety seconds, you actually can experience problems, deal with them, and go on very nicely if you don't fuel the thought that this should not have happened to you.

Managing emotions is a crucial skill and results in improved self-esteem and efficacy in living. Even if you are a very emotional person, you can work with your brain to shorten the time you stay upset. The next time you are in the grip of an intense negative emotion, try counting to ninety instead of counting to ten and give yourself a chance to decide if you want this unpleasant incident to be a short story or a feature film.

61 Try the Judgment Diet

It's impossible to judge the world into being a better place.

Judgment is like junk food. Oh, does it taste good! You think you can't eat just one potato chip? Try one judging thought. There is something so salty and crunchy about judgment thoughts. I could easily make a meal of them if it weren't for the annoying aftereffects.

Thinking someone is bad, or stupid, or mean is like eating popcorn. One thought leads to another and another until we are mindlessly gorging on a big bowl of negativity. Just as it is easy to watch a movie while thoughtlessly munching snacks, our minds can process our daily activities while endlessly thinking about who did what to whom and what a bad person this makes them.

In theory, we could still protect ourselves and watch out for problematic people even if we didn't add in the moral blame. That would work just fine, but people seem compelled to take it one step further. It is not enough that a person has hurt or angered us; we think we must file a mental indictment of their very character.

In a judging state of mind, we relish any term, diagnostic or scatological, that will define someone's shortcomings. Believe me, the mental health field is loaded with terms to call people who do things we disapprove of. But so is the rest of our culture. We can't get enough of negative categorizing.

The fascinating thing about this, however, is that categorical moral judgments do nothing to make things better. If they did, humankind's problems with life would have been solved by now. Hatred and rage have been used for millennia to solve problems, with plenty of violence to enforce these judgments. But at some point, we still have to solve the problem. Usually this means trudging to the peace table at long last or at least getting a grip on our resentments.

If judgment were not so gratifying at an emotional level, we could bypass it altogether and get on to the solution part. We could step back, analyze the issue, and find some kind of resolution. But when it comes to a contest between emotion and reason, emotion often wins. Reason is not nearly so much fun. The reward centers in the brain are unimpressed with long, nuanced lists of pros and cons. Reason may deal better with reality, but it won't light up your brain's emotional hotspots, nor will you get that sugar-rush certainty of how much better you are than those troublemakers out there.

When you fantasize about penalizing those who offend you, it costs your health and happiness. Judgment may make you feel full of power, to be sure, but the power to punish is a stress-filled power. You feel under constant threat.

How would you feel if you dropped judgment thoughts as soon as they arrived?

You would feel lighter, as if a burden had been lifted. You would feel like a gorilla had climbed off your back. You would start thinking about the things *you* want to do, not what others have done. The offending person would become an afterthought, while life's possibilities would open up. You would start thinking about you and your life instead of why everyone is not as you like. Instead of focusing on why this person was a jerk, you might ask, "How do I want this situation to turn out for me?"

If you give up junk food as a way to solve your frustrations, you will lose unwanted weight. It is the same on the judgment diet. If you are not always focused on what to judge next, you will find other more interesting and rewarding things to do. The weight you lose when you give up judgment thoughts will be the weight of the world. Just as you can never eat enough junk food to make your problems go away, you can never judge enough to make the world a better place. Besides, all you were ever responsible for was making the inside of you a better place. Shifting away from junk-food judgments will do just that.

62   Overcoming Social Anxiety

*Social anxiety comes from thinking that the point is to make
yourself liked.*

Most of us can get a little nervous in new social situations. That's only human.
But some of us get clammy with fear at the thought of a group of people. With
social anxiety, you get fixated on how others see you. You worry so much about
the impression you are creating that you stop experiencing your own experience. You feel scrutinized for the tiniest gaffe or flaw. Human interaction feels
like a pass–fail test.

Common advice for such situations is to not think about yourself so much
and pay more attention to other people. But when you are extremely anxious,
that can be hard to do. Anxiety makes you feel defensive, not curious.
Depending on your style, you might force yourself into strained sociability, or
you might miserably withdraw and wait for it all to be over.

Social anxiety comes from thinking that the point is to make yourself
liked. You get stuck in your head, and the only thing you notice about your
body is stomach-churning dread. Anxiety makes your mind overactive, so you
can't just shut it off. The answer to such anxiety is to move your energy from
worrying about the future to gently observing the present. You have to give
your mind another mission besides rating your likeability.

Moving into a mindful mindset shifts your social anxiety toward a calmer
direction. Mindfulness is a meditative technique wherein you pay attention to
what is happening inside you, noting it and letting it move through you much
as clouds pass across a sky. You don't judge it or nudge it; you just observe it with
calm matter-of-factness. The point is no longer to make yourself liked; the
point is to practice active meditation as you note with detachment what is
going on inside you and around you *right this moment*.

This is, of course, what people with anxiety rarely think to do. As soon as you feel anxious or self-conscious, you start haranguing yourself to do something. You tell yourself to act popular, look happy, or find someone to talk to pronto.

Instead, you could try something different. First, tell yourself you are doing a great job just standing there and breathing. Move your consciousness out of your head (where it makes you anxious), and concentrate on feeling your feet on the floor (where it stabilizes you) and the breath in your chest (where it centers you). Using the HeartMath technique, pretend that you have a giant nose on your chest and you are breathing through your heart, saying to yourself "calm" or "peace" on each inhale and exhale. Inhale through your nose and do long, slow exhales, which slow your heart rate. Remember a simple time when you felt safe, happy, and grateful. You are not pushing yourself, and you are not thinking of what to do next; you are just present, as serene as a sentient piece of furniture. If your mind starts to worry or judge, notice the thought without attaching to it, then quietly return to breathing through your heart and feeling your feet on the floor.

Look around you. Instead of you doing it, let the environment direct your attention. Do you notice anything that elicits interest? Is there something, or someone, that draws you to it? Give a moment to let action come to you rather than trying to generate it. Imagine you are your own company for the duration of the event. You are there for yourself, a pair of one. Tune in to your physical presence and notice your surroundings as you feel securely joined with yourself.

Shift your thoughts from judgment to love. Relate to the situation from your heart energy rather than your head energy. Instead of turning on your laser brain, lower your stomach and make yourself warm and pillowy. When you converse with someone, imagine that your heart energy is moving out into the space between you, meeting the other person's in the center where your heart-fields join. You are listening and participating, but your real aim is to notice and enjoy that silent confluence of energies that is going on between you. When the contact is completed, you peacefully return to experiencing your own wholeness. Then notice if anything else draws you toward it. In this way, you are using your imagination to comfort yourself instead of scaring yourself.

You can't fail with this approach. The goal changes from trying to be likable to focusing on that middle place where heart energies meet. One contact like this and the event is a success. That's all you have to do: Practice it one time with one person. Social contact thus becomes an opportunity for energy-giving meditation, rather than a draining performance. Everything's happening just as it is supposed to, which is how it feels when you lead with love. By imagining your heart energy meeting the other person's in complete acceptance, you are leaving no room for fear. Social anxiety becomes peaceful presence.

63 Master Your Machine Mind

To the machine mind, nothing feels as important as finishing that task.

Like all humans, you are of two minds. One is relational and experiential. The other is machinelike and driven to achieve. Both are needed to live fully, but they often get out of balance thanks to the bullying ways of the *machine mind*. Think of this as two siblings forced to live together in a close space, one of them dreamy and yielding, the other pushy and practical. It is easy for the pushy one to get the upper hand and run the show. It takes over because it can. And once it does, it convinces you that the important thing in life is to get things *done*.

Your machine mind—housed mostly in the left hemisphere of the brain—is all about task completion. It doesn't care how much stress it takes to get there. It likes nothing better than to set a goal and make it happen. It disdains the softer, more relational approach of the right brain hemisphere, seeing its emotional sensitivity as a drag on its own forward momentum. The machine mind cannot stand an obstacle, a delay, or a complication. It wants to drive straight ahead to the end point, and nothing better get in its way. Exasperation is the machine mind's reaction when other people want to get involved. When the goal is accomplished, the rush of satisfaction tells the machine mind that it was all worth it—even if it wasn't. This powerful sense of reward keeps the brain looking for the next thing to get done. The relational, experiential mind gets shoved to the back.

But what happens when machine mind is interrupted by a child who wants to play or a partner who wants to talk? What happens when a friend wants to get together and the machine mind is absorbed in a project? To the machine mind, nothing feels as important as finishing that task. Other things can wait but not finishing the job. Once you get caught up in that task-completion mindset, even our dearest relationships can feel like unwanted interruptions.

Caught in the cogs of your machine mind, you expect others to see how important our task is. You are impatient and irritated that others don't appreciate how hard you are working and what still needs to be done. Can't they see how busy you are?

Machine mind always feels like it is running out of time. Time is not something to be spent and enjoyed; it is something to be minimized and controlled because you never have enough to do all the tasks that machine mind comes up with. For machine mind, the shortest distance between two points is a straight line, a laser beam of intention. Living like this feels like a pressure cooker. You could always be doing things faster and more effectively. Life becomes an efficiency report. The meaning of life is reduced to finding which way takes less time to accomplish more.

The pleasure you get from task completion is powerful, but it has a short half-life. It does not linger to sustain you over the days to come. Enjoyment of task completion fades surprisingly fast, just like a drug high. That is because there is no heart in it, no warm, glowing feeling of connection to the world and other people. It is a sugar high compared to the sustaining nutrients of relational, experiential living.

It appears that we humans were made to replenish our emotional energy by enjoying the beauty of the world and rewarding interactions with people and living creatures. This relational mind is our home base, neurologically speaking. Originally, the machine mind was designed to protect those primary sources of relational energy by solving problems and getting things done. But the machine mind can be addictive. It can become more immediately gratifying to check things off a list than to tune into other people, animals, or nature.

In contrast to the straight-line style of machine mind, when you relate to the life around you, your mind naturally moves in waves and circles, repeating, revisiting, adding new color to previous material, seeing more in what has already been explored, broadening, deepening, and finding subtle connections. In this relaxed mindset, it is as though you are twirling tendrils of affectionate attachment around whatever has your attention. Relational mind is not about *getting there.* It is about fully experiencing this one immediate moment.

The next time you find yourself caught up in the stress of task completion, practice switching out of it briefly. Try to balance your life with deliberate moments of connection to your surroundings and other beings. Unhook from the driven feeling and let yourself bask in something you find heartwarming or beautiful. If that happens to be your child, partner, friend, or pet, even better. They may just be your real reason for getting all this done.

64 Stopping Self-Criticism

Its only goal is to steer you away from trusting yourself.

There's a funny thing going on in your head. You talk to yourself in ways you would never stand for from another person. The problem is that you don't seem to realize that you are the one doing the talking. Instead the critical voice you "hear" inside your head often sounds like the voice of ultimate authority. Worst of all, it has opinions about your self-worth that are based on ever-escalating expectations. Its fulfillment is a moving target. If you meet its demands, it raises your quota.

This head voice is like a crazy computer. When you get depressed, anxious, and feeling bad about yourself, you can bet it's running the ship. This onboard computer—or more accurately, this software in your computer—is an amalgam of rules, judgments, and knee-jerk reactions that you learned in childhood—likely from your EI parent. It is everything your mom or dad told you to make you into a perfect version of their ideal person. It is the same quest they have held for themselves, with better or worse results. And because they have probably never questioned their own self-critical voice either, they passed it on to you.

You do not recognize this voice as the source of your bad feelings. Instead, you think that following this voice will make life better. If you could only scale the heights it sets before you, you could finally be happy. You listen to this voice unquestioningly because you assume it has your best interests at heart. Why else would it keep weighing in on everything you think and do? It just wants to make you perfect, that's all.

If you knew real people who sounded like this voice, you would get away from them as quickly as possible. You might put up with their bullying if you had to, but in the privacy of your own mind, you might be thinking, *What a jerk!* However, when this voice comes from inside your head, you somehow have no perspective on it. You accept whatever it says as ultimate wisdom. So if it says one minute that you ought to stand up for yourself and in the next moment rebukes you for being too aggressive, you don't see its self-contradiction.

This is not the voice of conscience; it is the voice of criticism. The self-critical voice has no integrated, comprehensive philosophy, just a bunch of reactive judgments made up on the spot. It is not trying to guide you; it is trying to make you feel incompetent and small. Conscience wants you to act in accordance with your principles, which leads to improved self-esteem and confidence. Self-criticism is trying to get you to doubt yourself, pure and simple. It is not pointing you toward anything positive (although it implicitly claims to do so). Its only goal is to steer you away from trusting yourself.

Why? Because self-criticism is the internalized voice of tyrannical authority, and no tyrant ever wanted anybody to think clearly with self-confidence. Tyrants, whether in the outside world or inside your mind, just want to be the center of attention and the source of all decision-making. Whatever they say goes; it doesn't have to make sense. As the voice pushes contradictory goals that conflict with one another, you end up with a mind full of confusion and uncertainty.

To begin to get free of the self-critical voice, ask yourself if it is helping or hindering you in building the kind of life that you want for yourself. Is it helping you realize your dreams? Does its input give you strength to persevere? Does it give you productive new ideas that really make things better? Or does it carp at you nonstop, essentially kicking you when you are down? (Does that approach ever make someone stronger?)

This critical voice never knows when to lay off. In fact, the lower you sink, the more it overpowers. It seems to gain strength from your diminishment, just like any tyrant. It puffs up in direct proportion to your deflation.

The next time it speaks, notice what its values are. For instance, if it keeps berating you for making an error, it is espousing the value that people should be mercilessly punished for being fallible. Now ask yourself if that is in accordance with *your* values. Would you treat another person that way? Is it one of your cherished values that we should react to minor mistakes with insulting disre-spect and sweeping attacks on a person's character? Is it your conscious value that the only good people are perfect people? (I can think of a tyrant or two who had that idea.)

This voice comes from your past. You don't recognize the voice because it now speaks in your own voice, but originally it came from people outside your-self. As a child, you internalized many of the critical attitudes you heard and made them your own. You started talking to yourself the same way you were talked to or the same way you saw loved ones treating themselves. Either way, it works the same; someone showed you how to pounce on yourself when you made a mistake or didn't measure up.

The best approach to get free is to *externalize* the critical voice. Let's push those voices back outside where you can take a good, hard look at them. You will benefit from picking apart these swallowed-whole beliefs. Thank goodness there is a sensitive observer inside you that can tell the difference between being helped and being hammered. It can ask questions about what you really value and where you want to go in life. These reorienting questions are very effective in revealing the self-critical voice as the mixed-up, self-serving tyrant that it is.

At this point in your life, you get to decide how to treat yourself. If you treat yourself with pressure and criticism, you will feel bad and have little energy for accomplishing anything. If you treat yourself nicely with respect and guidance, you will have hope and energy to improve your life in a real way. The first thing to do is catch the self-criticism and realize that this self-blame is bad for you, not good for you. It will never improve you. The next step is to deliber-ately refocus your thoughts on what you want from life and what is most pre-cious to you. After a while, this positive refocusing will become your guide to life, and the tyranny of self-criticism will be voted out. In your inner world, you get to pick your leaders.

65 Seeking Perfection

*If you hold yourself to unrealistic standards, you will hold
the same unforgiving expectations for other people.*

Ideals can help you grow, but you have to be careful which ideals you pick.
Ideals are the handmaidens of perfectionistic thinking. Trying to live up to
exaggerated ideals can lead to stress, confusion, and depression. For instance, if
you are trying to be a perfect parent, spouse, or even worker, you can exhaust
yourself by worrying about whether you are meeting the ideal standard. This
ideal may actually be a hodgepodge of what you have heard, what you have
seen, or even how badly you want to be different from *your* EI parent. There is
rarely any questioning of these ideals, nor do you think of how they can affect
your relationships as you try so hard to measure up.

Idealism is the gateway drug for perfectionism, and the idea of perfectibility usually ends up with people getting punished in one way or another. If you
hold yourself to unrealistic standards, you will hold the same unforgiving
expectations for other people. If you are into perfection, even subconsciously,
you will always see other people as not trying hard enough to do things right.

The drive for perfection can start early in life, when a parent's frown or
emotional coolness lets you know you have erred. Although the parent may or
may not be intending this, you get the message that in order to be worthy of
love, you should be perfect. To make mistakes and cause disappointment is to
run the risk of a parent's emotional withdrawal, something no child can tolerate for very long. If love and closeness are tied to achievement, you will believe
that becoming perfect is the surest route to love and emotional safety.

If your parents held overly high standards, please remember it was never
about you in the first place. Your parents were children once too, just as

frightened of being rejected if they did not try hard enough to be perfect. You see your parents as authority figures, but they carry their own childhood fears as well. Trying to turn out a perfect child (you) may have felt like another chance for them to qualify for love and acceptance. No wonder they got so upset over your small mistakes. They were dismayed when you were not perfect, because your mistakes stirred the memory of their own childhood insecurities. They feared that your shortcomings might mean that *they* were bad.

Parents cannot teach kids how to be perfect, no matter how much they punish or reward. But children can feel good about little *improvements,* and parents can show them a good direction to shoot toward. When kids—or anyone else, for that matter—make mistakes, the healthy response is to figure out what needs to be done next and chalk it up to experience. In this way, you learn from experience, but without being saddled with irrational shame that you should have been perfect in the first place.

Instead of being perfect, you could enjoy your little improvements instead. It's all you could ever do anyway! Making small improvements here and there is much more realistic than trying for grand achievement every time. Why not drop that inherited false hope for perfectibility and see it for what it is: a punitive orientation to life that only gives out As or Fs. Making mistakes can never disqualify you from being a good person. As a matter of fact, it means you fit right into this very imperfect, very slowly improving world.

66 Find Your Pace

You can't prove your worth by getting a lot done.

Everyone moves at a different pace. Some of us are slow and methodical, while others are the jackrabbits in life, hopping from one thing to another in rapid succession. In modern culture, the busiest multitaskers are admired the most. They are so quick and industrious. They are so driven and distracted. The unspoken rule says you should be doing as much as you can as fast as you can. Nonsensically, you believe that the more you have to do, the faster you ought to be trying to do it.

You first learned to rush yourself in childhood. As a child, you are much slower than the big people around you, and your brain doesn't work as fast. You are told to hurry up, stop dawdling, and hit a pace that is unnatural to your young brain. Your parents might have taught you that taking all the time you need is equivalent to being bad or lazy. You carry this belief into adulthood, disregarding the fatigue and stress that otherwise could tell you that you are doing too much at once. You lose your normal sense of pace.

Your brain is designed to do one thing at a time, even though you can switch your attention rapidly among different things. This switching action costs you, however, because the part of the brain that decides where attention goes next is energy-expensive to operate. It takes a huge amount of energy to keep switching your attention in order to create the illusion that you are doing many things at once. The energy demand of all that brain-switching is what we call stress. It is the brain's way of telling you to slow it down.

Stress subsides when you get into a rhythm that feels comfortable—that is, the rate of processing your brain was designed to do. If you push yourself to go faster than that, you will feel stressed and your brain will become sluggish. So the more you have to do and the bigger the project, the more you should be slowing down to find your most productive pace for the situation.

When you try to push ahead of your brain, you soon will feel like you are about to explode. This is bad for your brain, your cardiovascular system, your stomach acid, and your adrenals. Stress hormones and elevated blood pressure are the body's way of saying you can't prove your worth through getting a lot done. Over time, your sensitivity to your brain's stress reaction can become so blunted and neglected that you no longer know how much time you really need to do something. Chances are you have not been allotting enough time to do things comfortably.

Why not cease this unnecessary self-pressure and find your true pace? Your best pace is how long it takes you to do something mindfully and comfortably. As you pay attention to your stress response, you will find a rhythm that makes tasks seem to do themselves. As soon as your stomach starts to tense up or the top of your head feels tight, stop and note the pressure you are experiencing. Take a full breath, exhale slowly, and slow down to find your pace.

As an experiment, break the task into bits, so that you can get the mini sections done easily and pleasantly. Or time yourself and see how long it really takes to do a job without stress. By paying attention to your bodily sensations, you can create slower, smaller units of effort that don't cause stress to your system. You will also find yourself more willing to do chores when rushing and pressure are no longer built into them.

Another way to find your natural pace is to double the time you think a task will take. If you think something will require a morning to do, plan two. It seems wasteful to do this because it goes against everything you've learned about being a good, productive person. But you will finally find out what your brain needs in order to do things with ease.

You may laugh at this, saying you don't have enough time as it is, let alone stretching it out longer. But by doing bits of a task over a longer period of time, your stress will decrease, and you will get as much done as before. It just won't all be compressed into one indigestible hunk of all-out effort. Time is not the problem; it is leaving it as one big job to be done in a rush. If you realize that it takes you twice as long as you thought to get something done, you will be content to chip away at it in pieces over a longer period of time. Your pace will feel comfortable, and you will still get everything done. If you find your pace, you'll find your peace.

Take the Right Approach for You

There's a secret to approaching life with less stress and more satisfaction. Try using self-awareness and self-acceptance to help you think more clearly for problem-solving and planning life on your own terms. With a compassionate attitude toward yourself, you stop fearing others' opinions and no longer waste your energy on unnecessary pressures. The secret is that there's no living well until you treat yourself kindly.

67 How to Approach Problems

A problem is just a reality riddle.

Problems are just nature's way of telling us we have run into reality. Yet they raise anxiety because they're usually unexpected.

Problems have their own lifespan, ripening until they reach a point where they get solved one way or the other. You feel pressure to solve them right away, but if you will give them room to fully reveal themselves, the solutions are often budding within the problems themselves. Problems need time to develop and unfold, and then solutions will come from using whatever is at hand. No radical new thing from outside the universe ever arrives to solve a problem. The solution will come out of the circumstances the problem sits in. It is like writing a story: all the letters you need are right there on your keyboard; you just have to put them in the right order!

Problems are made up of what already exists. Think of each new problem as a fresh pattern out of old materials—like a giant, slow-moving kaleidoscope that is in the process of tumbling into a new configuration. The sensation of solution occurs when the pieces once again fall into a pattern that makes sense. You cannot see the solution before it is finished forming no matter how impatient you get. Sometimes what you call a problem is nothing more than a shifting of reality, bits that will arrange themselves nicely when they are ready.

Calvin Coolidge once said that if ten troubles are coming down the road toward you, nine of them will fall in the ditch before they reach you. But when you get too anxious about what could happen, you end up running down the road to meet them, thereby picking a fight with what might not have become a problem after all. Acting before you can see the full pattern, you become part of the problem, pushing and resisting things that might have faded on their own.

You may have been trained to think of problems as always someone's fault, including blaming yourself. You would've learned this from an EI parent or any adults who responded to your mistakes with anger, blame, or judgment, as if all mistakes could've been avoided if you'd just been more careful. Such blame brings shame and makes you afraid of problems because you fear making a mistake. Blame keeps you focused on the problem, not the solution. But if you stop the blaming and instead take responsibility for your part in any problem— miniscule though it may be—you get closer to a solution because you are dealing with the one thing you do have control over.

Once the problem has been given time to evolve into something recognizable, you can start figuring out what to do. The best problem solvers are not people who rarely have problems. The best problem solvers just have a friendly, reality-based relationship with their difficulties. They do not take it personally when something goes "wrong." They might not know how to solve it immediately, but then they are not necessarily trying to. First they think it out and weigh whether action is needed or not. Because they are not alarmed by problems, they tend to come up with long-term solutions instead of impulsive stopgaps.

It works better to accept problems as inevitable and then play a game with yourself to see how calm and positive you can remain when they appear. When you are confronted with your next problem, tell yourself that the most important thing is that you continue to feel good. This will relax your mind and make you determined to maintain good self-esteem as you work on the problem's solution. Problems reveal their solutions if you calm down and give yourself time to think.

To quote John Wesley Kidd, "A problem is only a problem until we take action: Then it becomes a project." Knowing how you want your project to turn out is a huge help in guiding your problem-solving efforts. Always step back and ask yourself out loud what you are *really* trying to accomplish. Will your next action get you closer to that outcome or not?

Are problems a bad thing? You might as well ask if reality is a bad thing. A problem is just a reality riddle. The only way you get yourself into worse trouble is if you think you are entitled to not having the problem in the first place. A problem is not asking for your approval or disapproval. It is just showing you a piece of reality you did not see coming. If you can meet the problem with acceptance and curiosity, you may end up with a solution that sharpens your skills and makes you proud of what you accomplished.

68 Focus on the Outcome You Want

Focus on the outcome you want, not the problems you have.

Many of us are instructed early in life to think of others first rather than what we want. Given your experiences with an EI parent and possibly early authority figures (like teachers, religious leaders, or coaches), you might have learned that to be good, you should give in when your wishes run counter to someone else's. You may have been taught that it is rude and selfish to keep trying to get what you want. But very happy and successful people, on the other hand, never lose their ability to know what they want and to go after it. Mental health and well-being come from focusing on what you want.

Unfortunately, some parents think they are preparing their children for the reality of adulthood by teaching them to be compliant to others' wishes. What they are really teaching their children is to suppress their desires, not how to satisfy those desires through constructive problem-solving. They teach their children that cooperation means giving up what they really want instead of skillfully trying to affect the outcome in their favor.

Since adult life requires solving lots of daily problems—many of them involving other people—being taught to shut down puts you at a terrible disadvantage. You're likely to end up feeling resentful, powerless, and unable to defend your position. You may think that when stronger people push to get their way, you have no choice but to go along. You might believe your only option is to silently hope that other people will be nice enough to care about your feelings. When conflicts come up, you may revert to feeling helpless and victimized, not empowered. As a result, anxiety and dread take over when even normal conflicts arise.

Without a healthy sense of self-preservation, conflict brings highly uncomfortable emotions. Two of the most unpleasant-feeling reactions to conflict are anger and depression. Anger breeds resentment, and depression leads to hopelessness. For your own mental health and well-being, you really don't want either one. Fortunately, there is another response available to you, one that lifts you up instead of pulling you down.

What is the way out of resentfully giving in to what other people expect from you? *Focus on the outcome you want.* Pull back for a moment of reflection and ask yourself, "How would I really like this to turn out?" Remind yourself to focus on the outcome you want, not the problems you have. This immediately gives you a constructive goal and aligns you toward it instead of just focusing on the disagreement with the other person. You naturally then start thinking about the best way to move things in that direction.

You might be simply out of practice when it comes to thinking about solutions and outcomes once you get upset. Instead you may believe that getting upset is the normal and unavoidable response to any kind of conflict. It may be a natural first emotional reaction, but it is not where you want to stay. Your feelings are important, but they need not have the last word. It is up to you to take the next step and focus on the outcome you envision. Instead of slipping into helplessness and resentment, you could be dreaming up a solution you could be happy with.

But what if you cannot get everything you want? What if you have to make some concessions? If compromise is inevitable, don't get locked into resenting what you might have to give up. Instead, ask yourself, "What could I get out of this that would make it worthwhile to me to cooperate?" or "How could I turn this into something I would *want* to do?" It's the old principle of fair trade. I may not want to give up my bushel of wheat, but if you offer me a gold coin, I might change my mind.

Whenever you are ready to start, you can decide to reverse the self-defeating habit of resentfully giving in. You can change from feeling powerless and frustrated to becoming the agent of your preferred outcome. Practice outcome-thinking, and you will begin to generate ideas for a better solution—one that takes your needs into account too.

69 Challenge Your Negativity Bias

The brain is not really interested in your feeling secure or relaxed.

It's easy for our minds to dwell on negative things. Hurtful memories linger vividly, and fears stay strong. Apprehension often overwhelms anticipation, even if we're facing a positive challenge we chose ourselves. Why aren't we as likely to dwell on successful interactions or memorably trustworthy people? Why doesn't joy break into our emotional awareness with the same power as a jolt of fear?

The answer is our brain's natural tendency to fixate on anything that arouses fear or anxiety. It's called the *negativity bias,* an inclination well studied by psychologists. We come into this world with only a few innate fear responses, while the rest we learn on the job. But as we learn, we give disproportionately more attention and memory to the negative. Our negative experiences have an indelible effect with which positive experiences can't compete. They flash a warning light as soon as we are reminded of a painful past event. Post-traumatic stress disorder is a prime example, as are regrets about every thoughtless or embarrassing thing we ever said or did.

Negativity bias ensures that your perceptual systems react to threat in an absolutist way. If you see something potentially dangerous, 100 percent of your focus will rivet to that thing. Time will stand still as tunnel vision takes over. For instance, if you walked into a beautiful living room and immediately noticed a writhing rattlesnake on the rug, later you would be able to recall everything about that snake's movement and appearance but very few details about the room's decor.

This is why it can take so long to recover from emotionally painful experiences. Your brain keeps bringing up the memory, squeezing more and more anguish out of the details, as if it's afraid you'll forget and pet that rattlesnake the next time you see it or, even worse, bring it home with you. Even one major negative event in a relationship can reverberate for decades, long after the intervening good times have outweighed the bad by tens of thousands to one. It's good to know this so you can work to put disappointments in perspective and remember that difficult periods can occur between people in a context of otherwise strong devotion and trustworthiness.

This is not about denying the hurt; it's about not letting negativity bias throw out the baby with the bathwater. As James Doty says in his book *Into the Magic Shop*, just because one thing is broken, it doesn't mean that everything is broken.

The negativity bias has serious implications for parenting. Uninformed parents often believe that amplifying a punishment will make the child more likely to learn not to misbehave. Harsh corrections, like spanking or yelling, are thought to make the lesson stick. But thanks to the negativity bias, what gets imprinted on a child's mind is not the importance of good behavior but that parents can be scary.

Is there any upside to the negativity bias? Yes, because it makes you remember bad things that caught you by surprise and keeps you more alert in the future. The brain is not really interested in your feeling secure or relaxed. Feeling safe is no substitute for *being* safe.

Negativity bias can also help you remember neutral things. Because the brain lights up and pays close attention whenever anxiety is aroused, you will better remember something if you stick some apprehension to it. If you make up a little narrative that's slightly worrisome when you park, you'll never forget where you left your car. The same goes for repeatedly checking your surroundings to avoid getting lost. The reason we recognize when we've been going in circles is that our anxiety fixated on the environs as soon as we realized we were lost. As we return to that spot, our recall is perfect. Whether it's a mildly anxious situation or a major threat, your negativity bias will keep blinking a warning to help keep you alert and able to remember.

However, it is crucial not to let negativity bias rule your life. Although it was factory-installed as a warning signal, once it starts flashing, the negativity bias colors your past and limits your future. Fearful imaginings constrict your heart and energy, making you pull back even when it is perfectly safe to go forward. Your negativity bias can even harden into mistaken beliefs about the nature of life in general, keeping you in a contracted, defensive state.

Deliberate exposure to new surroundings and new people is the best way to counter the life-shrinkage that occurs when negativity bias is running the show. You can challenge your negativity bias through little adventures and explorations that can show you that everything new is not full of rattlesnakes. If you don't make a point to expand your horizons, the negativity bias will take over and flash increasingly stronger warnings about progressively smaller things.

Challenge your negativity bias to a debriefing. Thank it for being such a great warning system but ask it to let you experiment with a little more informed trust. Promise it you will be grateful for all the negative things it points out to you, but let it know that the ultimate decision to go forward must rest with your rational adult mind, not your primal fears. When you try something new and bad things don't happen, make sure to point this out to your negativity bias. Its inclination is to ignore anything safe or good, so you have to make sure it notices when things go well. You can negotiate with your primal brain to enrich your life in this modern world. Your negativity bias should function as a warning light, not your GPS.

70 Live Your Own Story

You can be yourself when you realize you can.

Trained elephants learn to accept leg tethers from an early age so that in adulthood, they can be controlled by ropes they could easily break. When young, they learn that, try as they might, the rope is unyielding and will not let them go. Now, several tons later in their development, they accept that earlier lesson as if it were still true. The elephant does not question the situation because in its mind, it is the same elephant it has always been. It does not realize that it grew up. Without an objective perspective on the relative strength of elephants and men, the elephant can only live what it earlier learned.

Humans also undergo a domestication process when they are young wild things. Little humans are taught a story about who they are and what life is about. These stories have often been passed down generation to generation in a family. Sometimes a family narrative is taught through actual stories and sayings, but other cues can be picked up from a mother's face or a father's stance.

Children are absorbent learners when it comes to family expectations. They want to please, and they want to belong. Children will go against their own instincts in order to increase their bond with the important people in their lives. In sociology, that is called learning the culture. Learning the family story—how one should think, feel, and act—shows children how to belong and how to predict other people's reactions. Following other people makes children less anxious and more secure. But while this may be adaptive while young, one can't live a productive, meaningful adult life based on a childhood story.

By trial and error, you discovered your place in the family story, and you began to take on your assigned role. In this way, you may have drifted into playing characters in your loved ones' stories. Not knowing any better, you might have figured this is all you are. Like the elephant, you may not understand how strong you have become. It is easy to underestimate yourself when you only see yourself as others saw you in childhood.

You may not like the story you are living, but unless you really examine it, you won't know why you feel so unfulfilled. Over time, you may come to realize that the part you're playing leaves you strangely empty and frustrated, even when others tell you that you should be happy. Soon you start wondering where your own story went.

Fortunately, each of us does have a true story inside, one that can come out when you realize you're an adult instead of a child. Your true story will give you a sense of excitement and hope when you think about the future. You will be able to identify life pursuits that raise your energy and sense of purposefulness. In this way, you seek your story of success.

But any story is only as good as the themes and values it expresses. Underlying themes are what the story is about. Without clear themes about what is precious to you, your life stories become a collection of episodes and vignettes, interesting at the time but lacking in plot. It is hard to feel excited and energetic about anything unless it supports values you believe are worthwhile. Without a theme-based story—without knowing what is important to you—you veer from pleasure to frustration and back again, never attaining the happiness that comes from knowing what you are trying to do and then doing it.

Might you be overdue for an update on your life story? Just like the elephant, you may still see yourself as weaker than you really are. You overlook your true power because psychologically you still feel young and weak. At a deep level, you may see yourself as a perennial child, seeking approval and security when you should be developing your adult identity.

To stop being a captive of family story, think about what is really precious to you in life. What do you find yourself gravitating toward? What topics catch your imagination? When you look at your life, what do you feel proud of? If you had to, what would you fight for?

This kind of self-reflection may take some time, but the results are worth it. When you wake up to your adult potential, a tremendous energy is released. You feel like you can do anything. Thin tether lines are seen for what they are, as you comprehend how big you have become. All the reasons why you can't be yourself give way to the revelation that you can be yourself when you realize you can.

If you don't define the theme and purpose of your life, it's easy to accept someone else's story about you. Only you can make sure you don't give your spirit away to anyone else once you are grown up. If you don't create and manage your own story, someone else may write it for you.

71 Life Coaching from Technology

Wisdom is invaluable wherever it comes from.

We can get unexpected life coaching from any source. The other day, I switched my car's clock back to Daylight Savings Time. But after changing the setting, the dashboard screen asked me if I wanted to save the change. It was the vehicular version of asking, "Are you sure?" But instead of appreciating my car's thoroughness in confirming my intentions, I found it irritating.

Irritation shows me that I'm not taking time to listen. I have discovered that when I get irritated, I am probably rushing in a way I'm going to regret. Irritation over little things usually means I'm expecting the rest of the world to read my mind and not delay me. If the one second it took to touch the save button felt like a nuisance, I was probably not very peaceful inside. Immediately, I realized the message from my car was not about setting the time at all; it was actually a signal to check my frame of mind. If that save button was getting to me, maybe I needed to slow down.

My car's blind spot indicator also reminds me of another powerful life lesson: don't claim the whole road as your own. Seeing where other people are and honoring their position leads to respect and good communication. But veering into the other driver's lane without even looking is like insisting on being right: The injury you cause might be your own. Every time we're tempted to take over, we could instead wonder what might be there that we can't see. It's good for our safety to consider other people.

My car is much less impulsive than I am. It has successfully taught me to set my intentions before moving forward because it won't start unless I first put my foot on the brake. This took me awhile to learn because I didn't associate starting to drive with pressing the brake pedal. But now I see how mindful this step is. I'm off to a much better start if I take a moment to be here now before going someplace else. To pause before going forward is the best way to proceed.

Like my car, my computer is a wise coach too. It reminds me that just because there are gigabytes of RAM available, it doesn't assume everything should be held in memory. My computer reminds me I have options every time I close out a document; it always asks me if I want to *save, cancel,* or *don't save.* I think I want to save everything before I close it out, but do I really? Maybe everything doesn't belong in memory.

Grudges are a good example of how putting things in permanent memory can be counterproductive. Resentment and self-criticism are things that don't deserve the save button. You may be tempted to create a file over every wrong committed by others, or yourself, but if you've learned your lesson, what's the point? Do you really want to use up storage on those negative thoughts? Learning to turn your thoughts away from blaming and bitterness is a crucial step in self-mastery. Besides, resolving the issue directly makes more sense than holding a grudge. Next time you're tempted toward resentment, maybe a button should appear with choices of *resent, transcend,* or *take constructive action.*

Your computer coach also reminds you not to disconnect without quitting first. Computers scold us if we shut things down abruptly. A little window immediately drops down to remind us there are proper steps to take before quitting anything. Computers dislike unfinished business and want you to tidy up before exiting. They know that anything involving separating or shutting down should engage in an intentional process. Don't just dump it, or you might regret it. Even computers realize that burning bridges is never a good idea. As much as you're able, finish up your interactions on friendly terms, and you won't have to worry about losing something important.

While computers and smartphones have many fail-safes and warnings, there is still one that needs to be invented. I'm amazed Google and Apple haven't come up with this yet. We need a pop-up before we send any email or text that says "This message could easily be misunderstood. Should you call them instead?" Now that would be a *really* helpful bit of technology. But until they get around to inventing it, we can remember to ask ourselves.

Wisdom is invaluable wherever it comes from, so let's remember the following lessons. Be aware that irritation might mean you are going too fast to keep your balance. Having memory capacity doesn't mean everything needs to be saved; sometimes it's good to let things go. Thoughtful delay is better than reactivity, as is setting your intentions before you start out. Look over your shoulder before moving into other people's territory. Prepare everybody involved before shutting anything down and try to leave all relationships on good terms. Even technology can be a life coach, showing you how to have a more peaceful and mindful life.

72   Crossing the Fear Boundary

Where you are is not who you are.

People like small, cozy spaces like a cat loves a cardboard box. Shrinking reality to a familiar size makes us feel safe and in control. It is an unusual person who really enjoys suspense in the business of living. For the rest of us, we want to hurry up and get things settled. Unfortunately, that can include our personalities and sense of identity too.

If you are like most people, you come to believe that you are your limits. It is very scary to leave the familiar because change feels like you would no longer know who you are. The cardboard box that you settled into now becomes your identity, to be held onto at all costs. Self-limitation feels safe.

Then when you are dumped out of your box, there is usually panic and desperation. How will you ever be okay without your familiar walls? You might not feel ready to cope with radically different experiences, and yet most people can and do. People cope pretty well. As soon as you stop trying to declare that things should not be the way they are and that happiness is only possible under certain conditions, you can expand your perimeter. Resilience is in your genes if you don't insist otherwise.

In fact, radical changes in life can often be surprising in how liberating they can feel. Suddenly you find out that your desperate circumstances are a kind of gift. You would never have taken those new steps if you had had the option of keeping up your safe boundaries. It can be exhilarating to find out that you can still function, that life goes on, even when you are shaken out of your box. Sometimes radical change can release such energy that you are almost giddy at being let out of the prison of predictability.

Apparently, there is a center in you that wants to grow and experience new things, even if a little risky. This part of you does not love a box. It has no limitations made of fear. It feels excited when opportunities come up in spite of the normal anxieties. There is fear, but there is also a lifting inside as your true self recognizes those things that are right for you. You feel more alive and alert.

Where you are is not who you are. There may be a larger self that you were meant to expand into, past the limits that your family or friends might have imagined for you. It is the greatest feeling to find out you are capable of much more than you thought possible. At the outset of a challenge, ask yourself this important question: "Deep down, does this feel like mine to do?" If the answer is yes, it does not matter how scared you are. Growth necessitates being scared; growth puts you in a spot outside your box where life is a lot bigger. Once you step over your fearful limitations, you will be amazed that you ever agreed to stay in so small a space.

73   Don't Call Yourself Lazy

Do you rate your goodness according to the amount of "work" you have gotten done today?

Many of us were raised in fear of being called lazy if we craved time for reading, TV, games, or other relaxing pastimes. We got the message that unless we were up and doing, fixing a problem, or otherwise progressing toward some measurable goal, we were somehow not being worthwhile. Just hanging out was not okay, and enjoying downtime was tantamount to shirking your duty. In many families, especially if your role was to bolster the self-worth of an EI parent, the pressure is on to always be achieving something that others agree is worthwhile. Being busy is the next best thing to being good.

If you grew up in such an atmosphere, this attitude can be internalized to the point where you subconsciously rate your goodness or badness based on the amount of "work" you have gotten done that day. If you conclude you haven't made enough effort, you might even lay awake at night worrying about what you didn't get done or what you have yet to do.

If this happens to you, pause a moment and consider your opinion of yourself at these times. I would bet that there is precious little compassion or interest in your feelings, circumstances, or needs and that you are treating yourself as only a means to the end of a job well done. At these times, the point of life may seem to be to check things off a list so that you can stop worrying if you've done enough to be good enough.

Needing rest and not wanting to do anything are not moral issues. You are not good or bad depending on how active or driven you are. You can get the essentials done and also enjoy your downtime. But if you criticize yourself whenever you feel like doing nothing, you never get the true replenishment that downtime is supposed to give you.

Your attitude toward your desire to relax says everything about your relationship with yourself. If you don't measure up to some imagined level of accomplishment, you may start mentally whipping yourself as though you were racing to come in first in some high-productivity stakes. You start riding yourself as hard as a hell-bent jockey in the Triple Crown. Then if you need to rest, you flog yourself with criticism. For this crazy mind-jockey, every decision to take a minute for yourself is a potential high-stakes loss.

But think for a minute. The stakes are not high. Most things are not emergencies. Our fear of laziness tells us we are in competition for our very worth, but we aren't. Staying keyed up and under the gun won't increase our moral standing one jot. In fact, the anxiety it produces is demotivating. Sometimes when you use a whip on a tired horse, it can make the horse lose heart and quit trying. When you add insult to injury by calling yourself lazy when you don't feel like doing something, you are doing the same.

Try a different approach. When you feel like doing nothing for a while, stand up for yourself against needless self-criticism. Talk back to criticism by saying, "Don't yell at me. I'm good!" You can usually get enough done to take care of the necessities and still have time to relax. You don't have to stay busy in order to be good. You already are.

74 Make Room for Space

Spaciousness is both energizing and calming.

Cleaning things out is hard because we are never sure what to get rid of. Everything we have was originally useful, beautiful, intriguing, or comfortable. But once it's in our home, our brains cling to it like flotsam after a shipwreck. We tell ourselves, "You might need that someday; better keep it," and hoarding gains its foothold.

It's true that if you keep anything long enough, you might find a use for it. But it can be a long wait for something to become useful. I used to feel dismay when I gave something away only to discover a use for it later. Now I just do the statistics. True, there may be an occasion when I could use that item again, but the odds of needing something I haven't used in years is astronomically slim compared to the high probability that someone else will enjoy it right now.

But the most important reason to get rid of things you're not using is that cleaning out stuff clears the mind and gives you breathing room. Manufacturers and advertisers tell you to fill space, not let it sit there. Their message is that more things mean more happiness. But space is very necessary in your home as a place to rest your eyes and open your soul.

The universe is made up mostly of space. How could we appreciate the stars if they glittered cheek by jowl and filled up the darkness? Would you rather receive a ring in a bag of junk or set off by the inky plushness of its own black velvet box? Could you enjoy your favorite piece of art if it left no open space around its subject? What about music? Would you enjoy a continuous onslaught of sound with no pauses? What's *not* there is as much a part of the experience as what is.

Advertisers know this well, and they always put plenty of visual space around what they are selling. They would never promote their new computer with pictures of it buried under a paper-strewn desktop, nor would they sell that new juicer by showing it stored in a cabinet full of unmatched lids. They certainly wouldn't push the latest fashion by photographing it in a closet of previous purchases. Instead, they sell the fantasy that these items will continue to have their own individual existence, retaining their aura of specialness forever. They know that space around an item sells the product and energizes the buyer. They never mention that graveyard of all our other impulse buys.

Everything we see around us takes a tiny bit of energy for our brains to process. When we have a lot of stuff, we waste mental energy just tracking things in our visual field. But when you look around and see open spaces, you get a sensation of opportunity. You feel lighter and more creative. You delight in what you do have because it stands out. Possessions then become inspirational instead of draining.

Open spaces attract us because the sensation of spaciousness is both energizing and calming. Spaces are where we recharge our batteries. Remember, every space you fill up will take a little of your daily energy to maintain. We can raise our overall energy by creating a little space around everything, and I do mean everything. When you go to declutter, make steely-eyed decisions about what is worth giving your space away to.

When you're cleaning things out, steer clear of sentimentality. Since an emotional reaction was what made you acquire it in the first place, it is not a reliable indicator. Letting your feelings be your guide means that you will end up with exactly as many things as you started out with because presumably there was some reason you bought them in the first place. Neither should you allow your imagination to come up with remote possibilities when you might need the item.

Accept the painful fact that if you give something away, you probably *will* find a use for it later. That does not mean you should keep it now. Instead describe *out loud* to yourself the specific reason you bought it originally, and then state out loud the exact reason why it needs to go.

There is always a reason why you don't use it, and you need to find it. You might have bought a shirt because you loved the color, but it never fit quite right. Or perhaps you bought a tool because it was supposed to be a time-saver, but you never learned to use it properly. Maybe you realize that short of that hobby project you'll never do, you will never need six of those widget things.

Regaining space lifts a burden we didn't know was there. Notice that wide, full breath you take when you can see a little of the wall behind your clothes or the extra shelf space in your storage area. That nice inhale is a sign of both relief and inspiration, evidence of room for new ideas in our life. Pretend it's spring and get going. There's no better time to energize ourselves by making space for right now.

75 The Art of Living

Commit to making your mistakes as beautiful as if they were intended that way all along.

I finally figured out what makes a great teacher. No matter what the subject, the teacher we remember gave us universal truths, not just specific facts. Universal truths hold their value across different situations, far beyond the classroom. Facts alone evaporate quickly, while universal truths sustain us for years to come.

One of the finest teachers of truth I ever knew was my art teacher, Devi Anne Moore. This teacher taught not just color and technique but also snatches of counseling and philosophy as needed to loosen up her students. She guided them through the labyrinths of creativity, instructing not just their eyes and hands, but their psyches as well. Devi was teaching art, but she could just as well have been teaching about life.

When Devi's students wanted to take on a challenging medium they had never tried before, she anticipated the discouragement that was sure to come from tackling something so new. So she delivered an attitude adjustment up front: "If you are going to do this thing, you have to decide that, no matter what happens, you're going to *make* it work." Just so there was no confusion, quitting was not going to be an option. Figuring out what to do now that you have ruined your picture was going to be an important part of the process, not the end of the process. No starting over with something easier. Take whatever happens and make it work. If it cannot be erased, change whatever needs to be changed to make it fit. Commit to making your mistakes as beautiful as if they were intended that way all along.

What a lesson for long-term relationships, not to mention parenting or any kind of creative pursuit. You are more likely to make it work if you refuse the option of throwing in the towel at the first mistake.

A frustrated student in my art class once complained that if he could finally get a drawing right after many attempts, why couldn't he get it right the first time? (If the ability was there all along, why all the false starts and mistakes?) Why not just go straight to the right lines in the first place? "Because all the learning happens in the mistakes," Devi pointed out.

When you overvalue perfection, it is easy to see errors as a waste of time. *Get it right the first time,* you think, *and finish it up.* What could be more efficient than that? But very complex, new tasks must be learned through mistakes, not mastered before you begin. You would have a hard time finding a professional athlete who thinks that because it is possible to break a record, one should be breaking records all the time. You learn deeply when you take the time to see what happens when you try it first this way and then that way. The immediate feedback of seeing a mistake is the quickest way to eliminate poor technique.

My art teacher also had a strange ambivalence about teaching her students techniques. She would show them techniques, but then she worried that her students would use them. "Don't become a slave to technique, or you'll do it that way every time." This was puzzling. Wasn't the point to do it right? And if someone showed you the right way to do it, wouldn't you want to do it that way every time? Not according to Devi. Every painting or drawing was to be approached freshly, finding its own natural starting point, on that day, in that moment. The feeling and tone of the picture dictated the next move, not a memorized list of steps. As soon as a student started feeling safe with using the same technique over and over in a stereotyped way, Devi was there to break it up. She had better not catch you sacrificing the organic integrity of your picture to the rules of a technique.

How much richer life could be if you used more originality and less technique! How many activities could benefit from the playful exhilaration of a fresh approach, new in this moment, rather than what has always worked in the past. If Devi insisted on the living spirit in our paintings, you could insist on reaching for the vital spirit of your life. If you find yourself doing too much of the same thing over and over, it may be time to ditch the technique, relax for a minute, and let the spirit move you.

Life is deadened when you worry too much about getting it right. Life loses its preciousness if you give up when it is not perfect. You will be happier with your world and yourself when you accept your mistakes as fleeting brushstrokes in the overall painting of your life. Instead of calling your mistakes demeaning names, you could take a page from another art teacher, Bob Ross, who famously said you should think of them as "happy little accidents," freely and innocently made, nudging you ever closer to what you are trying to achieve. You can make your mistakes work for your good. The most memorable learning occurs when you accidentally go the wrong way. Finding your way back and then seeking a new approach are solid methods, not only in art but in the art of living.

76 The Rest of Your Life

Getting older does not mean we stop having needs for personal fulfillment.

At my book signing some years ago, an older woman paused and sniffed disagreeably as she passed my book display. My title seemed to have hit a nerve with her, and she retorted that it was certainly too late for her to be thinking about who she was meant to be. Her unhappy face and downturned mouth told the whole story. She thought she was being realistic. What she was really being was depressed.

Getting older does not mean you stop having needs for personal fulfillment. You still have hopes and dreams, you still notice a good-looking person, and you still crave as much happiness as you can get. Your psyche, if truth be told, is not particularly affected by the aging process. You may slow down a little or gain a bit of wisdom, but in essence, you are eternally sixteen. The need to fulfill your desires is more real than anything the mirror might show you.

At heart, you are immortal. Your most basic psychological needs operate the same at seven or seventy. You experience your life as though you had all the time in the world. Telling yourself you are too old, or it is too late, or anything similarly self-limiting is not good for you psychologically. It creates bitterness. You can argue all you want that shutting down growth as you age is simply facing facts, but that kind of thinking is poison to your soul.

Why in the world would this be? Why does the inside of you want to continue to grow, while the outside of you gets older?

The answer is that you live in two worlds. There is a creation story from the mystical legends of Judaism that says that when the universe was brought into being, it split into two parts: the 1 percent world and the 99 percent world. The 1 percent world is the material, physical world that we know so well. When someone sighs and says, "That's life," they are talking about the 1 percent world. That was the world of the book-signing lady. It is the world that is ruled by physical aging.

The 99 percent world is a different story. This is the unseen realm of knowledge, joy, and inspiration. When you connect to that world, you have the happiest times of your life. The lucky among us keep an open channel to this storehouse of energy. Inventors, composers, and highly successful people have trusted in this world for centuries.

Psychological health in later years depends strongly on maintaining our connection with the 99 percent world. This world is the source of hope and optimism and a fair amount of our physical health as well. It knows that the mirror lies. It insists that we are going to go on forever—that a fact learned at age ninety is still worth learning, that a talent developed at sixty is worth spending time on, and that a love found at seventy is as precious a thing as it ever was. People who live with these beliefs tend to be happier, have fewer psychological symptoms, and live longer. Apparently, feeling immortal agrees with us.

When you cut yourself off from this 99 percent world because you think you are too old, too poor, too anything, you feel psychologically and spiritually impoverished. But once you reconnect with the 99 percent world, life is a feast again. The rest of your life can be viewed as a tour of exploration, not a prison term, once you start living like you are never going to stop.

Let's return to the book-signing lady. She was living her life with a plan to stop. She added up her age, looked in the mirror, and decided that it was time to start coasting to a halt. I know she thought she was being sensible, like making a will or planning her finances. (It does make sense to give the 1 percent world the attention it deserves.) But once that is done, it is a bad idea to store your psyche in such a barren little box of attitudes.

There is no time, no age, in the 99 percent world. It knows that your appetite for joy is more fundamental than external circumstances. It knows that life is not a dress rehearsal for death. If this is hard to remember at times, of course that's understandable. After all, we all have a book-signing lady inside us. But why not surprise her with the rest of your life?

Afterword

Now that you've finished this book, I hope you feel a little closer to the truth of yourself and the nature of life. Is your path a little clearer? In other words, instead of life feeling like a bossy EI parent telling you what to do all the time, can you now imagine it as a collaborative venture? If so, our time together has been time well spent. Actually, for me, it was well spent as soon as you considered taking the vital importance of your own self-care seriously.

Once you start caring about how you feel and what happens to you in life, you make yourself more complete, your life more fulfilling, and your relationships more sustainable. To me, evidence shows that we do better when we no longer suffer through life in an attempt to become good and instead see life as something to be enjoyed. I hope these insight-pieces have empowered you to value yourself just the way you are, without needing to make yourself into something you're not. You're not here to please any EI person, you're here to be you.

When you start caring for yourself with kindness and empathy, with the zeal of the sensitive parent you did not have, you can start living with a sense of the possibilities that have been yours all long. You are your most precious resource, all goodness and nothing unessential. Just follow your energy. Stop listening when anyone tells you to prove your worthiness through self-sacrifice—those days are over. Trust that life can show you what really matters. Trust that your life force is positive and active and that it knows what it needs. Align yourself with this spirit and your life will make sense.

When you make your life your own, it will never be hijacked by an EI person again. I hope this companionable book of insights will continue to give you the encouragement you need to create an authentic life that will be good for you and the world around you. Remember to look out for yourself—because you are so totally worth it.

Acknowledgments

This book is now a dream come true. But it may not have happened were it not for the unfailing encouragement of my husband, Skip. He saw the value of collecting these pieces and never let me off the hook when I day-dreamed about other ideas. Without his vision and frequent reminders, this collection might have stayed a future project. His willingness to support me in any way he could gave me the time and the faith I needed to pull this book together. I am so grateful to him for reading my work, giving me feedback, and keeping me pointed in the direction of completion. Most of all, I thank him for just being himself and thereby making me happy.

To my sister, Mary Babcock, I send all my love and deep gratitude for her willingness to read thousands of words and hundreds of pages as I struggled to edit and pick out the best pieces from twenty years of writing. Somehow, she managed to make it fun, always encouraging me with her praise and showing delight in the project but also being willing to tell me when a piece was not her favorite. Our many years of discussion and shared love of books made me sure of her instincts, and I cannot thank her enough for all the time she gave me.

Tesilya Hanauer has been the biggest promoter of my writing career. Were it not for our serendipitous meeting in Hawaii, all my thought and work on emotionally immature parenting might never have found its way to the kind of exposure and reader support it has enjoyed. Thank you, Tesilya, for taking a chance on me and for believing in the ideas.

Many thanks as well to Jennifer Holder for her excellent editing and sug-gestions, and to Susan Crawford, my agent, whose excitement about my ideas gave me my first foothold in publishing.

I also want to thank Peggy Sijswerda, the publisher of *Tidewater Women* magazine, who has given many writers a home for their work. Without the opportunity she gave me to be published, I would never have produced all these pieces plus many more. Peggy was a delight to work with, and her own writerly sensibilities maintained the magazine's consistently high quality. She always gave me the freedom to be myself and pick my topics. For this, I am eternally grateful.

Thanks, too, to Esther Lerman Freeman, who gave me much-needed support and advice along the way. My deepest gratitude as well to Lynn Zoll, Kim Forbes, Barbara Forbes, Judy Snider, and Arlene Ingram, who have always been so encouraging in their feedback on the pieces as they came out. As always, my best love to Carter, who brings me such joy and inspired all my parenting articles, and to Nick, who warms my heart and makes me laugh.

Lindsay C. Gibson, PsyD, is a clinical psychologist in private practice who specializes in individual psychotherapy with adult children of emotionally immature (EI) parents. She is author of *Adult Children of Emotionally Immature Parents* and *Who You Were Meant to Be*, and writes a monthly column on well-being for *Tidewater Women* magazine. In the past, she has served as adjunct assistant professor of graduate psychology at the College of William and Mary, as well as at Old Dominion University. Gibson lives and practices in Virginia Beach, VA.

More books to help you heal from emotionally immature parents

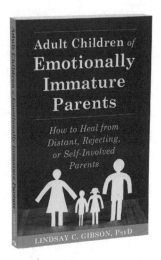

ISBN: 978-1626251700 | US $18.95

ISBN: 978-1684032525 | US $16.95

"Practical insight into a prevalent problem.... This book can be a source of healing for adult children of these kinds of parents."

—*Foreword Magazine*

"Gibson empowers those who have been raised by emotionally immature parents to fully reclaim their authentic selves."

—Kenneth A. Siegel, PhD, clinical psychologist